GW01311925

PIRATES, PANDEMICS
and
NATURAL DISASTERS

Interesting Facts and Challenges
about the Cayman Islands
and the Caribbean

John Clark

Pirates, Pandemics and Natural Disasters

CONTENTS

1. Caribbean Geography – Today   1

2. The Caribbean in Prehistoric Times   9

3. Caribbean History – Caribs, Columbus, and Colonisation   19

4. Pirates in the Caribbean   39

5. Rum and Slavery   61

6. Cayman Geography and Geology   77

7. Under the Sea   89

8. Interesting Creatures   113

9. Cayman History   131

10. Living in Cayman   165

11. The Power of Nature   183

12. Pandemics in History   199

13. The Coronavirus Pandemic in Cayman   213

Pirates, Pandemics and Natural Disasters

CHAPTER ONE

Caribbean Geography - Today

The Greater Antilles

The Cayman Islands, small as they are, are part of the Greater Antilles, along with five other countries – with two of them sharing one island.

See if you can match the countries to the letters on the map:

Haiti ☐   Cuba ☐   The Dominican Republic ☐

Puerto Rico ☐   The Cayman Islands ☐   Jamaica ☐

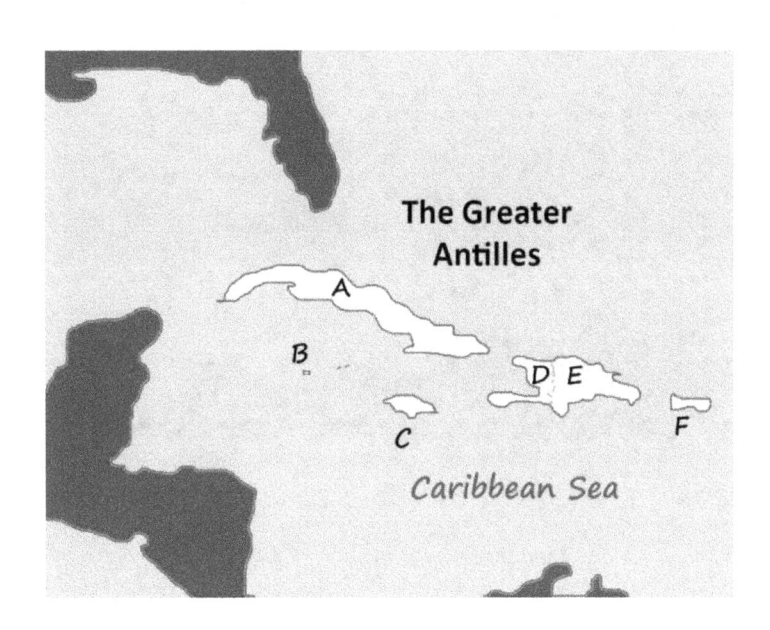

answers on page 8

The Lesser Antilles - The Windward Islands

In the Eastern Caribbean there are many smaller islands, together called the Lesser Antilles. They divide into two groups, **Windward** and **Leeward**. The ones shown in white on the map are the Windward Islands. The prevailing winds come from the southeast off the Atlantic Ocean and these islands face into the wind, hence the name. The Leeward Islands have been removed for the moment.

By some classifications, Barbados (B) is not a Windward Island, and Dominica (D), used to be the first of the Leeward Islands, but is now a Windward Island.

Given the initials, name the Windward Islands shown on the map.

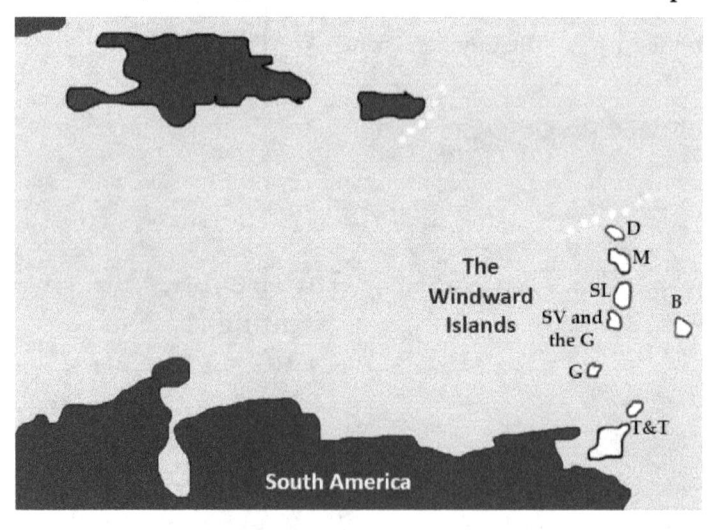

D....................   M........................   S..... L....................

S...... V..................... and the G...................   G...................

T..................... and T..................... (also, not 'officially' Windward Islands.)

answers on page 8

Lesser Antilles - The Leeward Islands

Most of the Leeward Islands are relatively small, but you can see that they finish off the arc from South America to Puerto Rico. Some of the countries are made up of several islands. The major ones are The Virgin Islands (some British, some U.S.), Montserrat, Antigua and Barbuda, Guadeloupe and St. Kitts and Nevis.

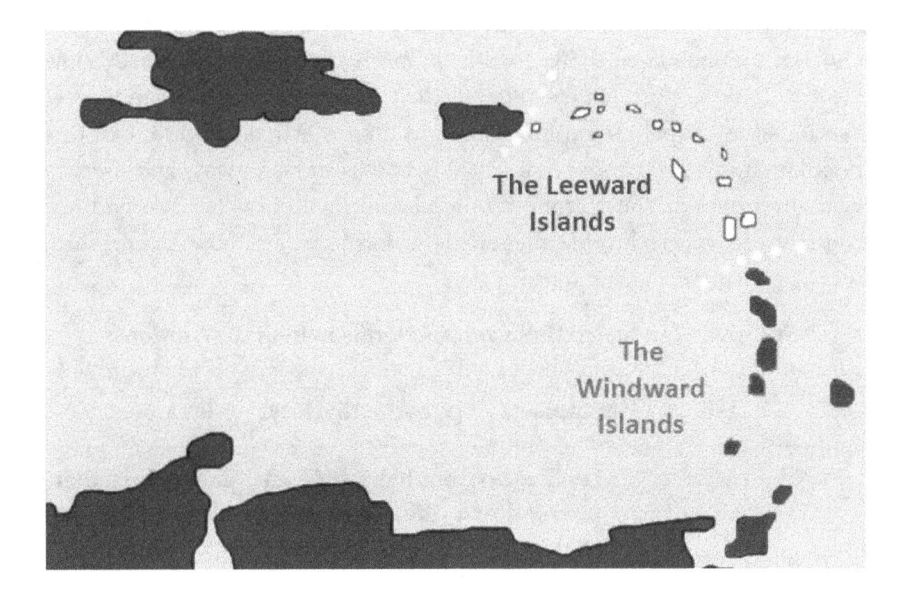

There is also one island that is shared between two countries. Half of it is called Saint Martin (which may not be pronounced how you think), and the other half is called Sint Maarten.

To which two 17th century naval superpowers do these two St. Martins belong?

answers on page 8

Volcanoes in the Caribbean

Volcanoes run all along the Lesser Antilles. There are volcanoes on Saba, St. Eustatius, Montserrat, Guadeloupe, Martinique, Saint Lucia, St. Vincent, and Grenada. Dominica has nine volcanoes!

Until 1995, Montserrat had been a quiet, tourist destination – but that year the Soufriere Hills volcano awoke after being inactive for two hundred years. The capital city of Plymouth and 20 other settlements were destroyed and left uninhabitable. It was difficult to escape as the pyroclastic flow destroyed the airport. Nineteen people lost their lives, and thousands were evacuated as eruptions continued off and on for years afterward. Out of a population of 11,000, more than 7,000 residents moved away, and tourism virtually stopped. The volcano erupted again in 2010, as tourism had just begun to recover. Today, life goes on in the northern part of the island, which was largely unaffected by the eruption.

See if you can match these volcano terms to their descriptions:

ash   **magma**   **pyroclastic flow**   **lava**

	lava, rocks, boulders, hot gas, and debris that pours down the sides of a volcano like an avalanche
	very hot, molten rock that is spewed out of the top or a vent of a volcano
	very hot, molten rock that is still underground
	fine particles of pulverised rock thrown out of the volcano, often travelling in the air like a cloud

answers on page 8

How Close is Cayman's Nearest Volcano?

The nearest active volcanoes to Cayman are all about 600 miles away. Central America has hundreds of volcanoes dotted along the Central American Volcanic Arc, but they are a very long way away from Cayman.

In other parts of the world there are lots of people living closer to volcanoes than you might think.

Here are some names of volcanoes, and the distances in **miles** from a nearby city.

Each city is home to between 600,000 and 1.6 million people! You might not have heard of some of the cities.

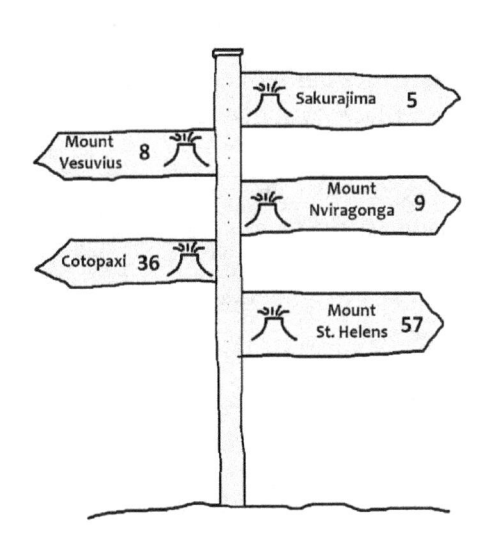

They are: **Naples, Quito, Kagoshima, Goma and Portland.**

Match each volcano to a continent.

Africa _____   Asia _____

North America _____   South America _____

Europe _____

In which <u>country</u> is Mount Vesuvius?   _____

answers on page 8

Find Grand Cayman

In 2019, half a million people arrived in Cayman by air, and if you have ever flown to Cayman, you will appreciate that the islands are mere specks relative to the vast water around them. The three islands combined have an area of just 102 square miles, whereas the Caribbean Sea is 100 million square miles; enough to fit 10,000 Caymans.

The picture below has nine Grand Caymans but only one is in the correct place. Which one is the real Grand Cayman?

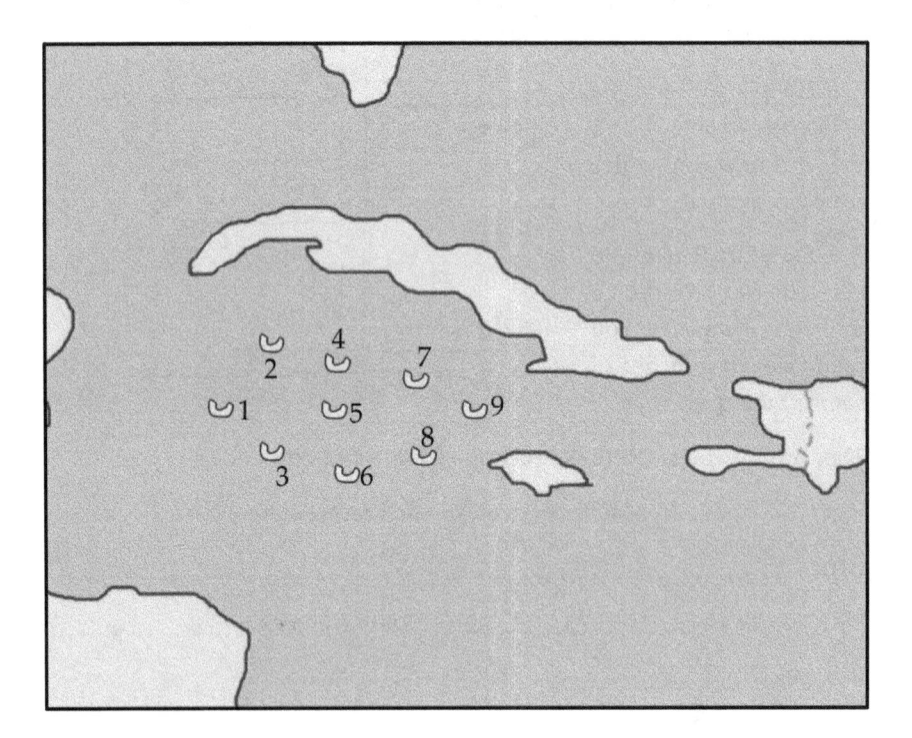

answer on page 8

Languages and Flags

There are two activities in one here. Identify the flag of each country and write their official language in the space provided. Greyscale flags add an extra level of difficulty. One country even based its design on one of the others!

green, white, red	blue, yellow, blue	blue, white, red	blue, white, red
....	....	....	Panama
....	....	....	....
red, white and black stripes	blue	pale blue and white	black, yellow stripes, green
....	....	....	....
....	....	Spanish	....
red triangle, blue stripes	blue, white, blue	blue triangle, red stripes	black triangle, blue and yellow stripes
....	Guatemala	....	....
....	....	....	....

Choose from: Bahamas, Barbados, Cayman Islands, Cuba, Dominican Republic, Guatemala, Honduras, Jamaica, Mexico, Panama, Puerto Rico, Trinidad and Tobago

answers on page 8

Answers for Chapter One:

Page 1. Haiti (D)   Cuba (A)   Dominican Republic (E)

Puerto Rico (F)   The Cayman Islands (B)   Jamaica (C)

Page 2. Dominica, Martinique, St. Lucia, St. Vincent and the Grenadines, Grenada, Trinidad and Tobago

Page 3. Saint Martin – (pronounced more like San Martan) - France   Sint Maarten-The Netherlands (Holland). By the way, it is worth looking up videos of passenger planes coming in to land above Maho Beach, Sint Maarten.

Page 4. Volcanoes   In order from the top: pyroclastic flow, lava, magma, ash

Page 5.   How Close?
      A. Mount Vesuvius - Europe (980,000 people)
         Cotopaxi - South America (1,6000,000)
         Sakurajima – Asia (600,000)
         Mount Nyiragongo – Africa (1,000,000)
         Mount St. Helens – North America (650,000)

B. Countries: Italy - the others are Ecuador, Japan, D.R. of the Congo, USA

Page 6. Number 5 is the real Cayman

Page 7. From top left:

Mexico (Spanish)	Barbados (English)	Dominican Republic (Spanish)	Panama (Spanish)
Trinidad and Tobago (English)	Cayman Islands (English)	Honduras (Spanish)	Jamaica (English)
Cuba (Spanish)	Guatemala Spanish	Puerto Rico Spanish and English (but 95% of Puerto Ricans speak Spanish)	Bahamas (English)

8

CHAPTER TWO

The Caribbean in Prehistoric Times

100 Million Years Ago

Earth looked very different 100 million years ago. The continents had not formed the way they are today, and even if the land were in the place where it is today, much of it would be covered by water because the sea level was much higher. In North America, west and east were separated by water, and where southern states are today the continent was submerged.

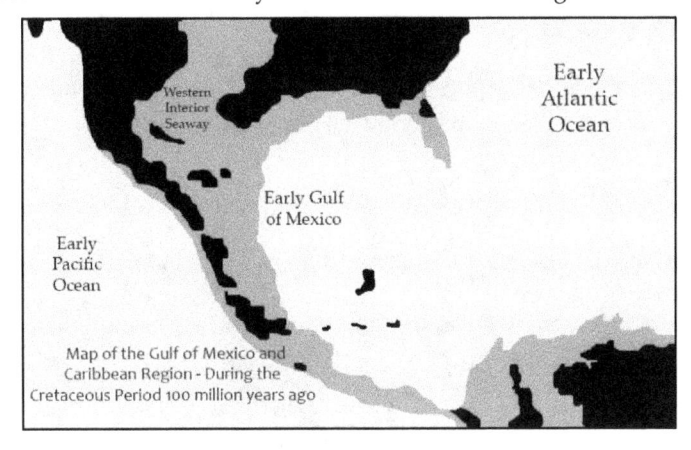

Map of the Gulf of Mexico and Caribbean Region - During the Cretaceous Period 100 million years ago

Circle the options that makes each of the statements correct:

a) Sea levels were so high that, at its peak, **one quarter/ one third/ one half** of today's land was submerged.

b) The temperature was about 5-10 degrees Celsius **hotter/ cooler** on average than it is today.

c) There was a lot of volcanic activity in **America/ Asia/ around the world**.

d) Bees and flowering plants began to **evolve/ die out**.

answers on page 18

Dinosaurs in Cayman - True or False?

1. The best place to find dinosaur bones in Cayman is in the **Crystal Caves** at North Side. **True or False**

2. Predators like Tyrannosaurus-rex never made it to Cayman, which is why there are so many fossils of stegosaurus and brachiosaurus. **True or False**

3. The wings of frigate birds are long and pointed and can span up to 2.3 metres (7.5 ft), the largest wing area to body weight ratio of any bird.

True or False

4. Frigate birds eat squid and fish and are direct descendants of the pterosaurs of the cretaceous period. **True or False**

answers on page 18

Mass Extinction Event

Most scientists believe that dinosaurs were all wiped out by an event that happened 66 million years ago. In fact, about three quarters of all living species on Earth became extinct. Apart from some crocodiles and turtles, nothing weighing more than a heavy suitcase survived! What is bad news for some is good news for others and many classes of animals started diversifying and evolving very successfully – particularly mammals.

What could possibly have caused such a catastrophe? Science is confident that it has at least one good answer. It was proposed in theory in the 1980s, and a discovery in the 1990s supported the theory - leading scientists to look in a certain place for evidence, which they found.

One of these mass extinction explanations is based on scientific evidence. Which one?

A. The whole of the **South Pole melted** – making the sea levels rise, and most animals drowned.

B. A **massive asteroid**, between 6 to 9 miles wide, crashed into the Earth. Fossil fuel deposits caused an explosion so great that millions of tons of soot were jetted up into the stratosphere and blotted out the sun for about a year. Animals starved. because there was no sunlight for plants to photosynthesize.

C. A few types of dinosaur contracted a **killer virus**. They were bitten by mosquitoes which then spread the plague to all the other animals.

answers on page 18

How Far from Cayman?

So, the dinosaurs were probably wiped out by an asteroid! The crater left by the asteroid is about 93 miles in diameter – as big as the circle in the bottom left corner of this map. Geologists looking for petroleum in the late 1970s were the first to wonder what they were seeing. Later, maps and samples started to reveal that what they could see was an impact crater. As recently as 2016, a scientific drilling project gathered the proof it needed that this was indeed due to an asteroid strike. The circular/oval shape of the crater can be seen on special photos taken by NASA.

Have a guess where the asteroid hit. This modern map has been divided into sections. **Pick one, for example D1**, and check with the answer on page 18. D1 is wrong, by the way. Grand Cayman is the small speck in B3.

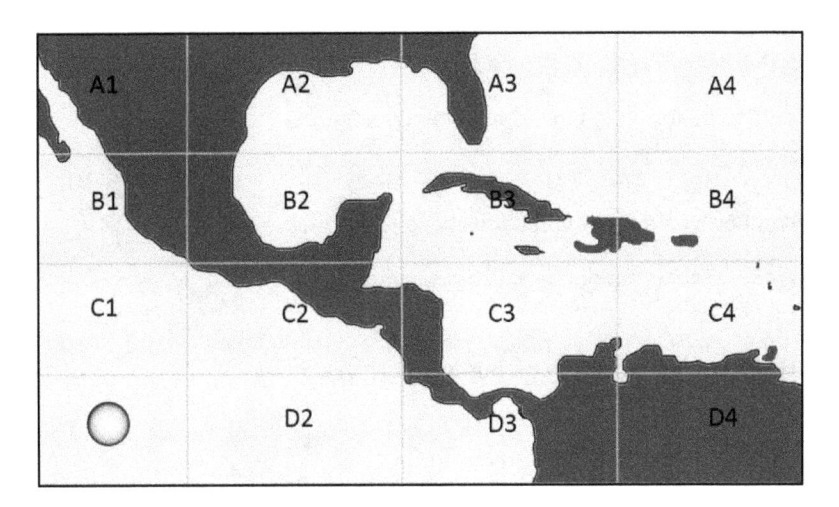

Scientists believe that the energy released by the asteroid impact would have been a <u>billion</u> times greater than the energy of the atomic bomb that destroyed Hiroshima.

answers on page 18

Are Stingrays Older Than Dinosaurs?

Cayman is famous for its stingrays. Some of the ancestors of our present-day stingrays may have witnessed the asteroid strike that ended the reign of the dinosaurs. Stingrays were swimming around gracefully in the Caribbean long before Tyrannosaurus rex was stomping the Earth. In fact, archaeologists say that stingrays have been around since the time of the diplodocus – about 80 million years <u>before </u>Tyrannosaurus rex.

What do you think?

Is this timeline True or False?

(It is best to read from the bottom to the top)

Today: **Stingrays** are still going strong.

66 million years ago: T. Rex and Triceratops become extinct.

68 million years ago: First T. rex and Triceratops.

145 million years ago: Diplodocus becomes extinct.

150 million years ago: Stegosaurus becomes extinct.

150 million years ago: First stingray. (Myliobatoidei)

155 million years ago: First Stegosaurus.

161 million years ago: First Diplodocus.

answer on page 18

14

Millions of Years

You might have seen some of these creatures in the waters or elsewhere around Cayman. Some have been around so long that they have survived *several* mass extinction events!

This list is supposed to be in order of how long they all have existed, but there is **one mistake**. One entry has got the number of years totally wrong - by about 200 million years!

Can you spot which statement is wrong?

Man has been around for less than 3 million years

Turtles have been around for about 220 million years

Lobsters have been around for about 360 million years

Dinosaurs (the big ones on land) were around for about 400 million years

Starfish have been around for about 450 million years

Coral has been around for about 500 million years

Sponges have been around for about 640 million years

answer on page 18

Map Match-up

The map below has some numbers where the names of places should be. See if you can work out which name corresponds with each number on the map. **Write the numbers in the boxes.**

Miami, USA   Mexico City, Mexico   Kingston, Jamaica

⬜   ⬜   ⬜   ⬜   ⬜

Havana, Cuba   Houston, USA

George Town, Cayman	Guatemala, Guatemala	Belmopan, Belize	Tegucigalpa, Honduras
⬜	⬜	⬜	⬜

answer on page 18

Distances from the Asteroid Impact

The x on the map opposite is Chicxulub, the place where the asteroid landed. The numbered dots are cities and capitals around the region. The table, below, shows how far each of these modern-day places on the previous page are from where the asteroid struck 66 million years ago. They are arranged from closest to farthest.

Description	Place	Nautical miles from Chicxulub
Capital city of a country with only an east coast		228
Capital city of a country of the same name		383
Capital city of a Spanish speaking island		425
Capital city of a country whose name translates as *great depths*		434
Capital of a small British dependent territory		476
The 8th largest city in the world		545
A city in the USA named after a native American tribe		593
The 4th most populated city in the USA		611
Capital city of an island famous for reggae music.		854

Complete the table by matching each description to a place indicated on the map.

answer on page 18

Answers for Chapter 2

Page 9.   a) One third of all land   b) hotter

c) volcanic activity was worldwide

d) bees and flowering plants began to evolve

Page 10. 1. False.   The oldest parts of Cayman emerged 30 million years ago. This might seem like a long time ago, but the dinosaurs as we know them had all been extinct for at least 35 million years by then! Some parts of the Cayman Islands are only 120,000 years old.

2. False. Sorry – no dinosaurs in Cayman. The islands are too young.

3. True.

4. False. The fossil record for frigate birds does go back 55 million years. Pteranodons, however, were neither birds nor theropod (dinosaur) ancestors of any bird. They were flying lizards.

Page 11.   B. The asteroid is the best explanation of the mass extinction event that killed the dinosaurs, although other ideas (not mentioned here) have merit too, including extended violent volcanic activity.

Page 13.   The asteroid hit in section B2, on the Yucatan Peninsula.

Page 14. It is TRUE. Also, be impressed by how long stingrays have lasted. Most dinosaurs were around for a few million years at most. Stingrays have lived for 150 million years!

Page 15. Dinosaurs (the huge and scary ones) were around for about 175 million years. They only date back as far as 230 million years ago, making them much more recent than many of our present-day sea creatures.

Page 16. Map. 1. Houston   2. Miami   3. Havana   4. George Town   5. Kingston 6. Tegucigalpa   7. Belmopan   8. Guatemala City   9. Mexico City

Page 17. Closest to farthest: Belmopan (7), Guatemala (8), Havana (3), Tegucigalpa (6), George Town (4), Mexico City (9), Miami (2), Houston (1), Kingston (5)

CHAPTER THREE

Caribbean History

The Caribs, Columbus, and Colonisation

The Caribbean gets its name from the indigenous people, the Caribs, who lived in the region in the 15th Century. It is believed that they were descended from the mainland Caribs of South America. The Island Caribs travelled and settled in Trinidad and Tobago, Barbados, Dominica and much of what we call the Windward Island today. The Caribs are represented by the dark areas of the map.

The Arawaks, and a sub-group of the Arawaks – the Taino, were in the region long before Columbus. They are represented by the map's white areas – particularly Cuba, Hispaniola, and Puerto Rico. Arawak is also the language that they spoke. By the time Columbus arrived many of the Arawak had been driven away from Hispaniola, leaving it inhabited mainly by the more aggressive Caribs.

Population Dispersion of Caribs (black areas) and Taino (white areas)

A population map like this is only a very rough guide. Every decade for a hundred years or more would have been different - as people explored and settled. Columbus was not the only person crossing the sea and discovering new land.

The Caribs – True or False

1. For centuries, European historians wrote that the Caribbean's earliest inhabitants were peaceful farmers who were wiped out by the ferocious Caribs. **True or False**

2. Throughout the 16th century, the Caribs were successful in fighting off the Spanish from many of the islands in the Lesser Antilles. **True or False**

3. In the 17th century, vast numbers of the Caribs were wiped out by European firepower, mainly by their cannons and muskets. **True or False**

4. It was reported that an Italian explorer was killed and eaten by Caribs in Guadeloupe in 1528. Historians think that eating humans was not for food, but as rituals associated with war. **True or False**

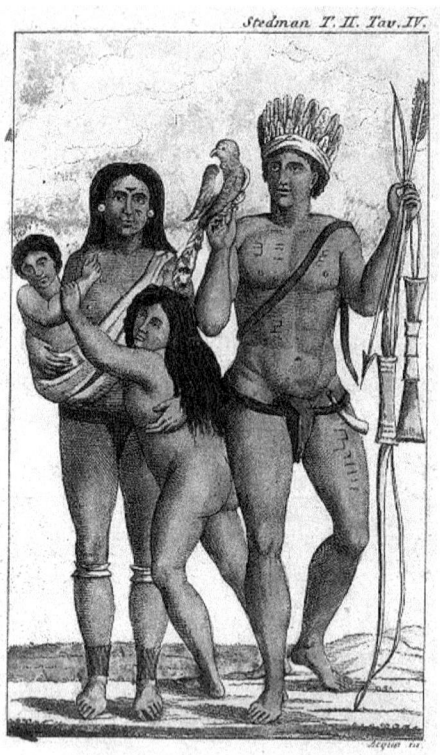

FAMIGLIA INDIANA CARAIBA.

Carib Indian Family by Stedman (1818)

5. In 1660, France and England signed a treaty with the Caribs stipulating that the Caribs had to evacuate all the islands of the Lesser Antilles and live on reserves in Dominica and St. Vincent. **True or False**

answers on page 36

Columbus in Europe

Until recently, the common belief has been that Columbus (Cristoforo Colombo) was born in Genoa, **Italy**. In 2012, a theory emerged that he may have been a Portuguese nobleman named Pedro Atíede. It may take time to ascertain his real identity, but we can refer to the explorer as Columbus – as this is the name that is purported to have been used, even by Atíede. 'Columbus' got the money for his famous voyages from the King and Queen of **Spain**. For his first exploratory journey he sailed two small, Portuguese-style caravels and a larger nau, which is perhaps better described as a carrack because *nau* is simply a word used in **Portugal** for ship. Some of the lands that Columbus found later became territories of **France** or **Great Britain**.

Can you find these 5 countries/kingdoms on this map of Europe?

ITALY   PORTUGAL   SPAIN   FRANCE   GREAT BRITAIN

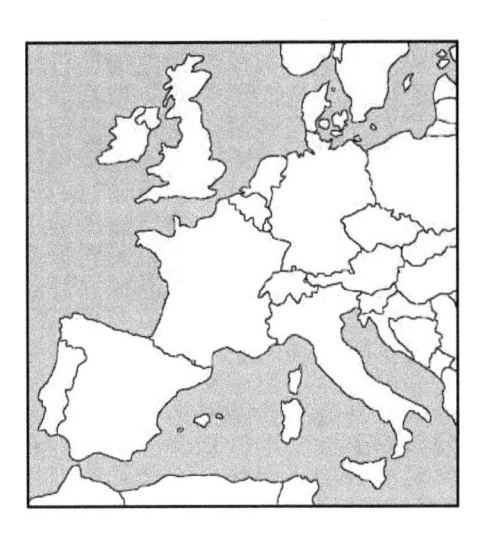

answers on page 36

Columbus Gets his Ships

In the 15th and 16th centuries, it was clear to Europeans that there were fortunes to be gained by whoever could find the best trade route to the East. Columbus had an idea that, as the world is round, it would be possible to head west across the Atlantic and get to China directly. He needed someone to pay for his ships and tried to convince the King of Portugal to finance his exploratory voyages.

The king turned Columbus away, preferring to find a route around the tip of Africa, heading east. Columbus tried to find backing from France and England, but they turned him down too, partly because they thought (correctly) that he had underestimated the distance, and that his drinking water would run out long before he got to the East – to Asia.

This solid line is how far Columbus would have had to travel to get from Spain to Asia. The distance that Columbus believed to be correct was much smaller than it really is, making China just a little past California (the black dot).

The distance that the kings of Portugal, England and France had considered WAS accurate (the arrow) - based on calculations that had been around for hundreds of years. They were right to believe Columbus would never make it. Luckily for him, there was a continent in his way, and he found land in the Bahamas (x).

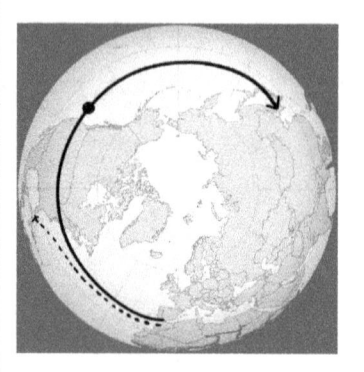

Undeterred, Columbus moved to Spain, and put his idea to Queen Isabella of Castile. Her priority at first was to recapture Granada from the Muslims. After that was accomplished, in 1492, she granted Columbus what he wanted – providing him with three ships. He equipped one large nau, a carrack-type vessel, and two smaller caravels and with a crew of 92 men in total, set off to find a passage across the Atlantic to Asia.

Columbus Heads for Asia

Columbus set sail in August 1492, unaware that it was a bad idea to be travelling into a tropical region in hurricane season. Although things might have gone very differently, he did not encounter any tropical storms (on that trip), and after sailing for thirty-five days from the Canaries he reached what is now San Salvador, in the Bahamas. There were already people there, so it cannot be said that he discovered it, but he was the first European to journey from Europe and find land in the Caribbean. The scene was set for him to become a wealthy and important man. From there he went on to discover other Caribbean islands and the continental landmass of the Americas.

If the Americas had not been in his way, the first part of Asia that Columbus might have reached could have been Japan.

San Salvador in the Bahamas is 4,000 miles from Seville, Spain.

How much further would Columbus have needed to sail to reach Japan?

a) another 2,000 miles

b) another 6,250 miles

c) another 7,750 miles

Landing of Columbus by John Vanderlyn, a Dutch painter. (1775-1852)

answers on page 36

Sizes of Ships

Columbus, at the age of 41, set sail to find a fast route to the East in 1492. He and his men were in three ships, the largest of which was a nau called La Gallega, though it is better known as the Santa Maria. The picture shows a modern-day cruise ship called the Celebrity Solstice. It is about 1,100 feet long and 200 feet high. Alongside it are sketches of 4 Santa Marias – on the same scale.

a) **Choose the ship** that you think is **closest in size** to Columbus' heavy, cargo ship, the Santa Maria. (A, B, C or D)

b) The cruise ship in the picture usually carries 4,000 people – passengers and crew. Estimate **how many men** were aboard the Santa Maria, Columbus' largest ship.

    i) 45   ii) 95   iii) 180   iv) 250

c) Columbus also took two smaller, faster ships. One was known as la Pinta, and the other, the Santa Clara, also had a nickname - la Niña.

What is the English translation of the Spanish term *la niña*?

answers on page 36

Hispaniola and Slavery

Hispaniola featured largely in the story of the Spanish conquest of the Americas. Columbus found it by accident on his first voyage in 1492, and Spain started a colony there the following year. In 1496, the Spaniards discovered gold and very quickly set up a system of enslavement to make the local people, the Taíno, work in the gold mines. Once the Indians entered the mines, they were wiped out by hunger and the difficult conditions. In less than twenty years, the Taíno population of about 400,000 was reduced to 26,000.

When Columbus' second fleet was returning home, Columbus loaded 500 slaves onto the ships to try to impress Queen Isabella. A great number of them died on the journey, and Isabella was angry with Columbus because she said that people in lands conquered by the Spanish were subjects of the Castilian Crown and should not be abused. She ordered them to be sent home to the Caribbean and freed. Although the Spanish monarchs published reforms to treat the Taíno people fairly, for the most part these rules were ignored in the colonies.

Enslaved Taino being forced to work the mines

Unknown artist. Public domain. British Library

Columbus sent 500 native people of Hispaniola to Spain as slaves. Estimate how many died on the journey.   a) 24   b) 109   c) 200

answer on page 36

Slaves Wanted – but only Catholic Slaves

From 1503, the Spanish began importing slaves into Hispaniola from Africa. Interestingly, because the Spanish were Catholics and were trying to convert the Amerindians to Catholicism, they were quite particular about which slaves they sent to the New World. Spain had just won a war against the Muslims but did not want to send Muslim slaves (Moors they had captured), to Hispaniola in case they spread the religion of Islam. The Spanish preferred to send only slaves of sub-Saharan African descent who had been born and raised in Spain as Catholics.

WANTED   NOT WANTED

A single sugar mill was established in Hispaniola in 1516 and, just ten years later, there were 19 mills. In 1574, a census noted that there were 1,000 Spaniards and a large number of slaves living on Hispaniola.

Estimate how many slaves?

a) 2,000 slaves   b) 4,000 slaves   c) 12,000 slaves

answer on page 36

World Events at the Time of Columbus

Just before Columbus:

c 1436: German goldsmith Johannes Gutenberg invented the printing press - combining metal movable type and a wine-press corkscrew method for pressure.

c 1430: Jan van Eyck and other European artists started painting in oils.

Columbus is Born:

1451 Cristoforo Colombo, (Columbus), was born between August 26 and the end of October in Genoa, Italy.

1481: The Spanish Inquisition begins in practice with the first auto-da-fé.

1488: The Portuguese Navigator Dias sails around the Cape of Good Hope

1492: Columbus sails west and finds the Americas

1494: Spain and Portugal sign the Treaty of Tordesillas, dividing the World outside of Europe between themselves.

1502: First reports of African slaves in The New World

1503-1506: The Mona Lisa is painted in oils by Leonardo Da Vinci

1506: Columbus dies

1513: The Portuguese mariner Jorge Álvares lands at Macau, China.

1517: Martin Luther questions the practices of the Catholic Church in his 95 Theses, igniting the Protestant Reformation of the Christian faith.

The Faces of Columbus

We take for granted how easily our image may be captured, stored and made public. Since the camera was invented, famous people have posed for photographs or have been snapped by the paparazzi, sometimes when they did not want to be seen. Since cameras have been built into mobile phones anyone can take a picture of a person, wherever they happen to be, and the internet is awash with pictures of people – famous and not so famous. We can even take selfies. In the 16th century, capturing the visage of a person was not that easy – not even that of a celebrity.

Back then the only way to capture a likeness of someone was to employ an artist to make an engraving, a woodcut, or a painting, which, for the subject, meant sitting for hours and paying a lot of money. In some cases, where there are several portraits of the same famous person, closer inspection reveals that some paintings are merely copies of the first one.

Navigators such as Columbus, Vespucci and Magellan were at sea for many years – exploring, so it cannot have been easy to capture their images. However, there was some time between Columbus' first and second journeys when he stayed at a palace in Spain and might have had an opportunity to have his portrait painted. Unfortunately, because he had returned from that voyage without finding gold, or spices and silks from the Far East, he was probably not considered worthy of such an honour.

The portraits on the next page all purport to be of Christopher Columbus, or Cristoforo Colombo, the navigator and explorer. The one on the left is supposed to have been painted by Sebastiano Luciano Piombo, but that artist would have only been 21 years old when Columbus died, and only took up painting later in life so it is doubtful that it is an authentic painting from a 'live' sitting. The inscription behind Columbus was added later, and it is possible that whoever added it also signed the work as Piombo to make it more valuable.

The painting in the centre was commissioned by Thomas Jefferson of the USA and was painted around 1788 – almost three hundred years after Columbus. It was a copy of a copy, and to save money, Jefferson had asked for it to be painted by an artist who would "work cheap". We cannot really trust that to be a good likeness of Columbus.

The image on the right is attributed to Ridolfo Di Domenico Bigordi, also known as Ridolfo del Ghirlandaio, but it must have been painted posthumously, about forty years after the death of Columbus. It is likely that Ridolfo worked from an earlier painting and used a little guesswork. Unlike today, when the faces of celebrities are all over the media, in those days very few people would have known exactly what Columbus looked like, and so very few would have been able to comment on the accuracy of the likeness of Columbus in the portrait.

Catholicism Spreads to the New World

Although the story of the conquest of the Americas is very much about what could be taken *from* the region, such as gold, silver and sugar, the Spanish monarchs very much wanted to take something *to* the region – Catholicism.

The Taino people were indigenous to the region and populated Puerto Rico, Cuba, Jamaica, Hispaniola and other islands. They already had religion and a hierarchical structure of government. Their religion had a supreme creator and other gods responsible for hurricanes, crops, fertility, war and disease. Caribs, generally a more violent people, were also living in the region. They too had several gods - and an evil spirit who needed to be kept pleased. The local inhabitants were forced by the Spanish to give up their beliefs and convert to Catholicism.

The Spanish were Roman Catholics, led by the Pope. At that time there were other Christians who were not Catholics, mainly Orthodox Christians, who had separated from Catholicism about 450 years before Columbus' voyages. Shortly after Columbus, some other Christians broke away from Catholicism and, because they objected to its greed, overstated ceremony, and corruption, became known as Protestants.

Portrait painting of Pope Alexander VI (Pope from 1492-1503) by Cristofano dell'Altissimo of Italy.

Thousands Tortured

Catholicism was the only religion allowed in the New World in the colonial era. It was hard to resist Catholicism. Although it is based on the peaceful teachings of Jesus Christ it was harshly imposed in Spain for over 200 years. Jews and Muslims were forced to renounce their religion or were driven out of Spain by a system called the Inquisition. It was also easy to accuse others of heresy, and thousands of people were tortured and were burnt at the stake in public shows of power by the Church and the Catholic monarchs.

Today, 90% of Latin Americans are Christians, mostly Roman Catholic, with around half being practising churchgoers. In Spain, the dominant religion is also still Catholic Christianity – but, according to the Spanish Centre for Sociological Research, fewer than 25% would claim to be practising adherents.

Amerigo

Surely, if you had a whole continent named after you, people would know your name. Not necessarily. North America, Central America and South America are all named after an Italian explorer and cartographer, and hardly anyone has heard of him!

Columbus had set off to find a route to the Far East. He thought that the land he had found was the eastern edge of the Orient. Amerigo Vespucci, an Italian financier and navigator, sailing for Portugal in 1502-1503, demonstrated that it was an entirely different land mass. Although many cities and the country of Colombia bear Columbus's name, Vespucci gets the grand prize – he got a whole continent (America) named in his honour in 1507.

It is interesting, but not so unusual, that Vespucci's first name was chosen for the honour rather than his surname. Most people have heard of Michelangelo, Donatello and Raphael but do not know their family names. Using first names was customary back in those times. If they had used Amerigo's surname, the USA might now be called the USV - the United States of Vespucci.

There have been many places named after people - often saints, or kings and queens. **See if you can identify the person after whom these places were named.**

Country / Dependent Territory

| Colombia | Bolivia | Mauritius |
| The Philippines | The Cook Islands | Bermuda |

Also, consider how many places (not counting pubs) that you know that are named after Queen Victoria, King George, or Prince Albert – all first names by the way.

answer on page 37

Sailing and Ships

1. Which three of the following are NOT names of sailing ships?

sloop   dhow   schooner   bruiser

carrack   pinto   draught   ketch

2. What is the name of the traditional sailing vessel of the Cayman Islands?

a) lugger   b) croc   c) catboat   d) goatee

3. Which three of these words are NOT sailing terms?

beat   jab   line   heel   luff   coulomb

tack   jibe   jib   canter   reach

4. Match the names of these four sailing ships to their pictures:

galleon _____

junk _____

cutter _____

longship _____

answers on page 37

Columbus Crossword

Across

3. What Columbus set up for his brother to run on one of the islands (6)
6. The movement of the tide out to sea (3)
8. The last voyage of Columbus was his .... (6)
9. By heading west, Columbus hoped to find a quicker route to the Far ...... (4)
11. A tribe, native to the Caribbean (6)
12. The country that paid for Columbus' voyages (5)
13. The French speaking neighbour of the present-day Dominican Republic (5)
14. Fruit composed of an inedible hard shell and a seed, which (usually) can be eaten (3)
16. Initialism used for southwest (2)
18. The branch of mathematics that was used by Eratosthenes to calculate the circumference of the Earth, before the Common Era (8)
19. How many men Columbus left behind in Hispaniola after his flagship ran aground (5)
21. A Portuguese word for ship, and the class of ship of the Santa Maria (La Gallega) (3)
24. Over 100,000 inhabitants on Hispaniola were killed by these (foreign types) within twenty years of Columbus' arrival (8)
27. Columbus would have recognized dios, dio or deus as the word for this (3)
28. Potentially killer disease, often following the word 'Spanish' (3)
29. More than thirty of these animals joined Columbus on his second voyage (6)
32. The island that is now shared by Haiti and the Dominican Republic (10)
35. The penalty imposed by Columbus on local people who did not collect enough gold (5)
36. The aftermost and highest deck of a ship (4)
39. One of the three countries that turned Columbus away because he had underestimated how far he would need to travel (7)
41. Diary or record kept by the captain of a ship (3)
42. The left-hand side of a vessel, or direction from a vessel, when facing forward (4)
43. To decay or decompose – a problem for wet wood (3)
44. Nickname of the small ship, the Santa Clara, which had a crew of only 18 men (2,4)
45. A triangular sail that sets ahead of the foremast of a sailing vessel (3)
47. To make ready a boat or ship for sailing (3)
48. The aft-most part of a ship or boat (5)
49. A staple food in 15th century Americas and the Caribbean, and their source of flour (5)

Down

1. At, near, or towards the stern of a boat or ship (3)
2. A journey towards a specific mission or goal (5)
3. Fettered, like Columbus was when he returned to Spain in 1500 (7)
4. How many times Columbus' original flagship crossed the Atlantic Ocean (4)
5. The female saint after whom Columbus' flagship was named (5)

Caribbean History

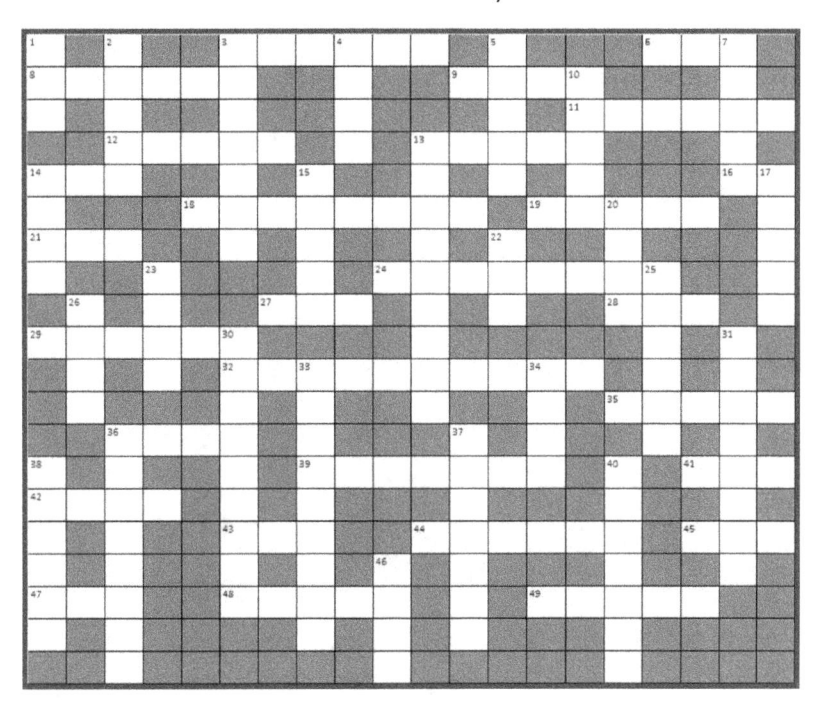

7. Protein-rich food eaten in Mesoamerica long before the arrival of Columbus (5)

10. The people who were native to Hispaniola (5)

13. This tropical event damaged Columbus' ships in 1502 (9)

14. Number of stranded crewmen still alive when Columbus returned one year later (4)

15. The Spanish word for friend (masculine) (5)

17. See 22 down

20. Often difficult to see, marine obstacle on which many ships have met their fate (4)

22. The 'fourth continent', the Americas, came to be known by this name (3,5)

23. Tall, upright post that supports the sails and rigging on a ship (4)

25. Columbus sent 500 of these to a horrified Queen of Spain (6)

26. A precious metal Columbus expected to find (4)

30. Molluscs that sank two of Columbus' ships, leaving him stranded in Jamaica (9)

31. Columbus' religious denomination (8)

33. How many centuries, prior to 1492, it had been known that the Earth was round (9)

34. What Columbus and his crew did not see for about 70 days (4)

36. Country on the Iberian Peninsula (8)

37. Where Columbus landed, assuming it to be the Far East (7)

38. 3-dimensional object – similar to the shape of the Earth

40. The nationality of Columbus (7)

46. Nautical measure of speed (4)

solution on page 37

Answers for Chapter 3

Page 20. Caribs – True or False
      1. True, but if Caribs had written history books, they may have mentioned the role that Europeans played in wiping out the indigenous people.
      2. True (poison darts were particularly successful weapons).
      3. False. They were wiped out by the diseases the Europeans brought with them, to which they had no immunity, and by malnutrition, forced labour and slavery.
      4. True. The English word *cannibal* is even derived from the word Carib.
      5. True.

Page 21.

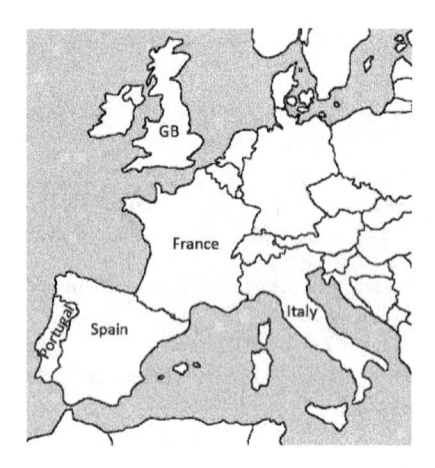

Page 23. Another 7,750 miles! Columbus had calculated the circumference of the Earth to be 25% less than it really is. Even worse, he imagined Asia to be wider – making Japan further east, closer to Europe. This mistake would have resulted in another few thousand miles of travelling – and death to his crew from lack of water and provisions.

Page 24. a) D. The Santa Maria was 161 feet (49m) long   b) 45 men (the 2 smaller ships had crews of only 18 men)   c. girl

Page 25. 200 died on the journey

Page 26. There were 12,000 slaves on Hispaniola

Page 32. Christopher Columbus, or in Italian, Cristoforo Colombo (Colombia), Simón Bolívar (Bolivia), Prince Maurice van Nassau (Mauritius), King Philip II of Spain (The Philippines), Captain James Cook (Cook Islands), Spanish sailor Juan de Bermúdez (Bermuda)

Not only are there numerous cities across the British Commonwealth, there are states, lakes, islands, rivers, mountains, waterfalls, harbours, docks, hospitals, museums, railway stations, parks and a myriad of other places that are named after Queen Victoria.

There are about 50 George Towns or Georgetowns around the world, including over 30 in America and of course the capital of the Cayman Islands. The state of Georgia is named after King George II.

You might think that the Canadian province of Alberta is an obvious answer for a place named after Prince Albert, but it was actually named after Queen Victoria's fourth daughter, as was the city in Saskatchewan.

There is a lake in Uganda/Congo, numerous bridges, a concert hall, and a museum (the Victoria and Albert), named after Prince Albert.

Page 33. 1: bruiser, pinto, and draught   2. catboat   3. jab, coulomb, and canter

4. galleon (c)   junk (d)   cutter (a)   longship (b)

Page 34 and 35 Crossword.

Across   3. colony   6. ebb   8. fourth   9. East   11. Arawak   12. Spain   13. Haiti
14. nut   16. SW   18. geometry   19. forty   21. nau   24. diseases   27. god   28. flu
29. horses   32. Hispaniola   35. death   36. poop   39. England   41. log   42. rot
43. La Niña   44. jib   46. rig   47. stern   49. maize

Down   1. aft   2. quest   4. once   5. Maria   7. beans   10. Taino   13. hurricane
14. none   15. amigo   17. World   20. reef   22. New   23. mast   25. slaves   26. gold
30. shipworms   31. Catholic   33. seventeen   34. land   37. Portugal   40. Italian
45. knot

Pirates, Pandemics and Natural Disasters

CHAPTER FOUR

Pirates in the Caribbean

The most famous pirates are those who operated in the Caribbean from the middle of the seventeenth century – the 1650s. We tend to picture pirates as bearded rogues, sailing wooden galleons fitted with big square sails, firing cannons and muskets, and fighting with swords. However, there were pirates in other places around the world long before those times, and unfortunately, there are still pirates roaming the seas today.

Pirates are robbers who attack people at sea, in boats and ships. They are likely to be violent and kill people who try to get in their way. They have little regard for human life – they just want to get rich by stealing things of high value.

Shortly after Columbus discovered the New World, Spain started mining gold and silver on the islands and the mainland, and there were precious gems to be taken from the area too. Spices and silks were being transported from the East, across Mexico, and then onto ships sailing back to Spain. Ships across the entire Caribbean Sea were either laden with treasure or carried goods that could be sold for very high prices. These ships made great targets for pirates, but they generally travelled in groups and were usually very well protected.

The Treasure of the Spanish Main

The Spanish Main (dark line) was the name for all the coastal lands along the mainland of Central and South America that Spain had conquered. Soon after Columbus discovered the Americas, Spain began to systematically plunder everywhere in the region, and took back to Spain all manner of goods and treasures. Because of the tremendous riches shipped from it, the Spanish Main was a ripe target for pirates and privateers.

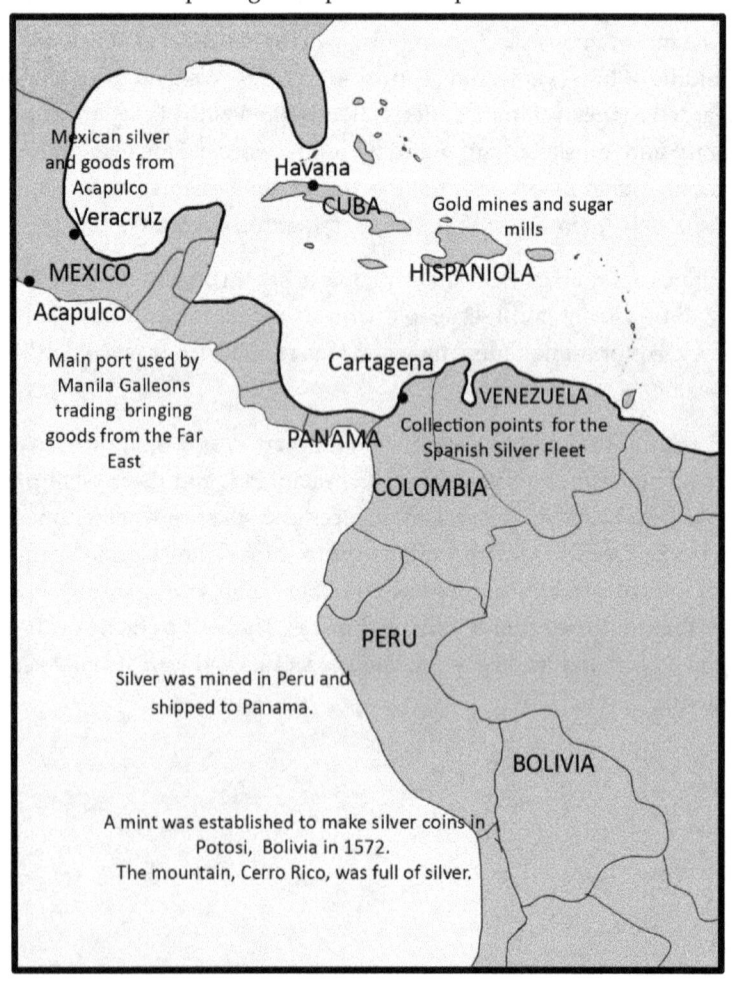

The Manila Galleons

From 1565 the Spanish set up a shipping route from Manila, in what is now the Philippines, to Acapulco, making one or two round trips per year. These carried all kinds of luxury goods, spices, dyes, and silks all paid for with the silver from the Americas. These were transported overland across Mexico from Acapulco to Veracruz, and then shipped across the Atlantic to Spain in galleons – the big wooden ships from the pirate movies.

Pieces of eight

Spanish silver coins dollars. They were called pieces of eight because each coin was worth 8 Spanish reales.

Bolivian Silver

Deep in South America – a long way from the Caribbean, is a mountain called Cerro de Potosi - nicknamed Cerro Rico (Rich Mountain) because it was so full of silver. The Spanish set up a mint in Potosi in 1572 to make their coins – 'pieces of eight.' Potosi was the major supply of silver for the Spanish for over a hundred years. The silver was taken to the Pacific coast by llama, shipped north to Panama City and then transported by mules across to the Caribbean side of Panama. There, it was loaded onto ships bound for Spain.

From the 16th to the early 19th century, the Spanish Main was the point of departure for enormous wealth that was shipped back to Spain in the form of gold, silver, gems, spices, hardwoods, hides and other riches.

Privateers

Not all ships that attacked and robbed other vessels were pirate ships – some were privateers. Some countries would sponsor mercenaries to use privately owned ships, armed with cannons and crewed by violent men, to harass and plunder ships of other countries in times of war. The British Admiralty would issue 'letters of marque' giving them permission, so that the men could not be charged with piracy. The ships and the men aboard them were both called privateers. Sir Francis Drake was a privateer operating on behalf of Queen Elizabeth I.

Drake was a hero to the English but a pirate to the Spaniards - to whom he was known as El Draque (The Dragon). King Philip II was said to have offered a reward of 20,000 ducats, over $5 million by modern standards, for his life.

Drake's ship, the *Golden Hind* had between 18 and 22 guns and cannons.

Enemy ships, captured by privateers, and their cargoes, could be sold - and the 'prize' money was shared between the ship's owners, sponsors, captain, and crew. Some of the proceeds also went to the sovereign – for example, the Queen of England. All the countries with significant navies authorised privateers in times of war. It would be very tempting for privateers to continue with this very profitable business and turn to piracy between wars.

Captain Morgan – Sir Henry Morgan

Born in 1635 in Wales, 'Morgan the Terrible' was active as a privateer in the Caribbean from around 1663 (aged 28), until 1671 (aged 36). When Spain and Britain had a falling out in 1667, Morgan was given a letter of marque by his friend, the Governor of Jamaica, which meant that he could attack Spanish ships and bases without being criminalised as a pirate.

Morgan went on to attack Spanish towns in (what is now) Cuba (1662) and Panama (1666), which made him rich. He also used the Cayman Islands as a staging post before his attack in 1668 on Puerto Principe, Cuba. In 1669, Morgan attacked Spanish cities in Venezuela and stripped them of their wealth, sinking several ships in the process. Morgan was becoming a rich man and soon owned three large sugar plantations in Jamaica.

By 1670, Morgan was in command of 36 ships. In 1671 he attacked Panama City, burning the Spanish owned city to the ground. Unfortunately, a peace treaty had been signed between England and Spain the previous summer and Morgan found out about it too late. The Spanish wanted Morgan punished, so he was arrested and taken back to England. Morgan was a hero in England and was later cleared of the charges.

Henry Morgan the privateer from the "Pirates of the Spanish" cigarette card by Allen & Ginter

While Morgan had been away from the Caribbean, the privateers, without their inspiring leader, had been reluctant to fight. Also, England was now at war with Holland and there was a danger that the Dutch navy might be able to seize England's lucrative sugar plantations in Jamaica. In 1674, King James II knighted Henry Morgan and sent him back to Jamaica as Lieutenant Governor to protect the country.

Sir Henry Morgan died a rich man, in 1688, aged fifty-three. Pirates and privateers from around the Caribbean attended his state funeral in Jamaica, protected from arrest by an amnesty. He was buried at Palisadoes Cemetery in Port Royal, Jamaica, -but only stayed there for a few years! In 1692, an earthquake struck Port Royal and two thirds of the town sank into the sea, into Kingston Harbour – including the cemetery and Captain Morgan's grave.

Sir Henry Morgan, Lieutenant Governor of Jamaica

Take a guess:

How many slaves do you think Henry Morgan owned at the time of his death?   a) 9   b) 54   c) 88   d) 129

answer on page 60

The Golden Age of Pirates (1650 to 1720)

Times were very hard in England in the 1600s. The country suffered from plague, crop failures, religious upheaval and severely cold weather that lasted for well over two hundred years and is known as the Little Ice Age. Apart from the usual blaming of Jews, Muslims or even Protestants for catastrophes and disease, the persecution of women as witches came to a peak in the 1640s. This period must count in English history as one of the most difficult periods in which to survive. People left England in droves, many, such as the Pilgrim Fathers headed for America.

The Mayflower landing at New Plymouth, 1620

In London, especially, there was massive overcrowding and unemployment. There was no hope. Young men might have to work seven-year apprenticeships before they could make an independent living. Going to sea gave people a chance to escape and may have been especially appealing to young adolescents. Honest seamen earned very little, and life on board ship was harsh. In contrast, piracy not only offered them a chance to get rich quick but also a chance to be someone – to have power. But not everyone who worked on a ship had volunteered for that trade.

Becoming a Pirate

In the 17th and 18th centuries it was legal for the Royal Navy to hire press gangs to draft recruits by kidnapping young men from their homes in the middle of the night, or to get them drunk and abduct them when they passed out. Often their families never knew what had happened to them. Life was hard for these sailors, who were beaten often. Life expectancy for men pressed into service was no more than two years. Many crews mutinied against their officers or just surrendered when threatened by pirates. Then they became pirates themselves. If they ever returned to England they would be hanged for the crime of mutiny, so it was better to live as a pirate.

Life was hard for the pirates but not as bad as one might expect. Men had more equality aboard a pirate ship than they ever had in the navy. Pirates elected their captains. Because many sailors had been press-ganged and forced to work on a ship against their will they could sympathize with slaves and there are many reports of pirates attacking slave ships in the Caribbean so they could free the captives. Black and white pirates fought and lived in equality, side-by-side. Women also joined the crews wearing women's clothing most of the time and men's clothing whenever they anticipated battle. Pirates of the Golden Age lived by a code that divided the loot from a haul fairly among all the crew. This was a far better deal than the low wages they were paid in the Royal British Navy.

Most of the sailors spent their loot quickly in the towns that catered to pirates, but some held on to their money and managed to rise in status to captain. Some even became landowners and governors. There is little or no evidence of pirates burying treasure, contrary to what is portrayed in films and books, including the classic *Treasure Island* by Robert Louis Stevenson.

Buccaneers

The term *buccaneer* is from the Caribbean Arawak word *buccan*, a wooden frame that Tainos and Caribs used for slowly roasting or smoking meat. When the French moved into the area, they referred to local people using that style of cooking as boucanier. The word became associated with the French privateers more than the food.

Buccaneers lived on the Caribbean island of Hispaniola and its tiny turtle-shaped neighbour, Tortuga, in the 17th century. At first, they lived as hunters, but later the governors of Caribbean islands paid the buccaneers to attack Spanish treasure ships. Although raids began in this way, with official backing, the buccaneers gradually became out of control, attacking any ship they thought carried valuable cargo, whether it belonged to an enemy country or not. The buccaneers had become true pirates.

The Spanish had their own name for meat cooked this way, and a version of it is quite widely used today.

What is the modern-day word, derived from the Spanish, for cooking meat in the style of the Taino, Caribs and buccaneers?

— — — — — — — —

answer on page 60

Famous Pirates

Thousands of pirates were active between 1650 and 1720, and these years are sometimes known as the 'Golden Age' of piracy. Though this Golden Age came to an end in the 18th century, piracy still exists today in some parts of the world, especially the South China Seas.

Some of the pirates from the Golden Age did not operate in the Caribbean, so they are not so well known. Henry Avery was probably the most successful pirate of the era, even though he only ever plundered two ships. In 1695, he and his men captured two ships in the Indian Ocean, one of which was the Grand Moghul of India's treasure ship – full of gold and jewels. This was enough for a majestic retirement, which he and his crew spent in the Caribbean.

Four of the five famous pirates mentioned in the next few pages were born within six years of each other, with Anne Bonny being a few years later. Four of the pirates featured in this chapter are close enough in age to have all attended the same school. Imagine that!

The flag of the English pirate Jack Rackham, also known as Calico Jack.

Black Bart – Bartholomew Roberts

Born May 17th, 1682   Died in action in 1722, aged 39

Black Bart was the most successful Caribbean pirate in terms of the sheer number of ships he captured. In his mid-thirties, the Welshman was second mate on a slave ship, The Princess, which was captured by pirates and Roberts was forced to join the crew. After only six weeks, the pirate captain was killed, and the crew voted Roberts to be the new captain.

Roberts' first raid was one of his best. In a harbour off the north coast of Brazil he stole a ship laden with treasure, ready to set sail for Portugal. In the harbour there were 42 ships and their escorts – two huge man-o'-wars, each with 70 guns.

'Captain Bartho. Roberts with two Ships' – engraving 1724

Roberts boldly sailed into the bay as if he belonged to the convoy and took over one of the ships without making any fuss. He soon extracted the information he wanted from the ship's master, who told him which ship was carrying the best prize. He promptly attacked the richest ship and overpowered the crew, capturing the ship. Roberts and his men sailed away in the two ships, and the well-armed but slower vessels could not catch them.

Black Bart's strategy was like that of other pirates. He kept capturing larger ships and refitting them with better weapons. He liked to use the name *Royal Fortune* for whichever ship had newly become his flagship. Roberts is believed to have taken 400 ships over the three years that he was active. In 1721 he captured a very large frigate off the coast of Africa and mounted her with 40 cannons. With a fleet of four ships, he was almost unstoppable, and his men became very rich.

Wealth is only useful if you can live long enough to enjoy it – which was always a challenge for pirates. In February 1722, a man-of-war called the Swallow had been sent to hunt down Black Bart near a slave-trading centre off the West Coast of Africa. Though he might have been able to escape, he chose to fight. Unfortunately for Roberts, early in the battle his throat was ripped to shreds by grapeshot fired from the Swallow. He died and was thrown into the sea (as he had told them to do) by his crew. Without their leader, his 152 men soon surrendered. Of these, 52 Africans were sold back into slavery and 37 sent to the West Indies to be indentured servants. Some, who managed to prove that they had been forced into piracy, were acquitted. The remaining 54 were hanged.

Black Bart has been immortalised in books and in movies. Most notably, he is mentioned in *Treasure Island* by Robert Louis Stevenson and in the movie *The Princess Bride*, 'Dread Pirate Roberts' is also a reference to him.

Two of these books were written by Robert Louis Stevenson. Which two?

Kidnapped   Shipwrecked   Robinson Crusoe

The Strange Case of Dr Jekyll and Mr Hyde

answers on page 60

Blackbeard

Blackbeard (Edward Teach) was born between 1678 and 1683

He was killed in action in 1718, aged 35-40

Blackbeard was an Englishman who had probably been a sailor on board privateers in Queen Anne's War. He joined Benjamin Hornigold and from 1716 engaged in piracy with him until Hornigold retired the following year. Soon after, Teach captured a slave ship, named her the Queen Anne's Revenge and furnished her with 40 cannons and a crew of 300 men.

Edward Teach (Black Beard), *Walking the Plank*, from the "Pirates of the Spanish" cigarette card by Allen & Ginter

Blackbeard was such a fearful sight that many of his victims gave in without much of a fight. He was tall and broad-shouldered and wore a long coat and knee-length boots, with pistols draped around him 'like a bandolier'. He had an impressive black beard, which he twisted and tied with ribbons. In battles, slow burning matches were entwined in his plaits or hung from his hat. Unlike some other pirates, there are no stories of Blackbeard being brutal or ruthless. It seems that much of his success was due to his fierce appearance.

Anne Bonny and 'Calico Jack' Rackham

Anne Bonny was born in County Cork, Ireland, between 1697 and 1700. Her mother was a servant and her father, William Cormac, was a lawyer - her mother's employer. Later, Cormac left his wife and moved to London with his daughter, Anne, who he dressed as a boy, and where she trained as a law clerk. When Anne was in her teens, Cormac, Anne and her mother moved to Carolina.

Anne's father became a wealthy man as a merchant and plantation owner, and he wanted Anne to become a respectable lady. She, however, fell in love with a sailor – a small-time pirate called James Bonny. Cormac disliked Bonny – who had one eye on acquiring Cormac's estate. Against her father's wishes, when she was just sixteen, Anne married James Bonny. Cormac disowned Anne, and in 1718 she and her husband left for New Providence, a pirate haven in the Bahamas.

John Rackham, known as 'Calico' Jack because of the clothes he wore, was a quartermaster working on a pirate ship commanded by Charles Vane. Rackham caused division amongst the crew when Vane refused to attack and plunder a much larger ship, and the men thought they had all missed an opportunity to become rich. The outcome was that the men supported Rackham as being the new leader, so he and most of the men took Vane's ship, leaving him with a small crew and the smaller of his two ships. Rackham spent a while plundering ships between Jamaica and Haiti, and sometimes the Leeward Islands. He then accepted a pardon in 1719 and moved to New Providence, where he met Anne Bonny.

Meanwhile, in the Bahamas, James Bonny was acting as an informant for the governor of the island, leading to many arrests of pirates. This turned Anne against her husband who mingled with pirates in taverns. She became the lover of 'Calico Jack' Rackham, who offered to pay money to James Bonny if he would divorce his wife. Bonny refused, threatening to beat his wife. 'Calico Jack' returned to piracy, with Anne joining him as part of his crew.

Rackham, Bonny and Mary Read

Mary Read was born in England and spent some of her childhood in the guise of a boy. Before she was born, her mother was married with a son. Her mother's husband died at sea around the same time that she had been having an affair with another man. The late husband's mother knew nothing of the affair or the pregnancy and offered financial support for her grandson. Mary was born and her half-brother died in the same year, so Mary's mother pretended that Mary was her son so that the boy's grandmother would continue paying support. This ruse worked throughout Mary's childhood and into her teens.

After that, Mary worked as a servant, a foot-boy, and then joined the British military, working on ships disguised - or at least dressed, as a man. She fell in love with a Dutch soldier, and together the two bought an inn in the Netherlands – presumably to the bewilderment of her shipmates. When her husband died soon afterwards, she returned to military service with the Dutch navy, again as a man, before quitting and boarding a ship for the Caribbean.

When Mary's outbound ship was captured by pirates, she willingly joined their ranks, as Mark Read. Those pirates were captured in 1718 but Read, presumably, claimed that she had been forced to join the crew and accepted the King's pardon. Read, again as a man, took a commission as a privateer around 1719 but joined the crew of that ship in mutiny shortly after, becoming a pirate again. In 1720 she met up with the pirate Calico Jack Rackham, Anne Bonny's lover. Bonny was in Cuba giving birth to her first child at that time but joined the ship as soon as she could afterwards.

At first, Bonny and Rackham both believed that Mary Read was a man. It cannot have been long before Mary had confided in Anne and revealed her secret. Jealous of the bond between the pair, Calico Jack threatened to kill Read – forcing Bonny to reveal that this hard-hitting pirate was a woman. No other crew member was aware of her secret, until Read fell in love with a cabin-mate.

Calico Jack, Anne Bonny and Mary Read were mainly active in the waters around Jamaica, on Rackham's sloop *William*, which he had stolen from the bay in Nassau while it was at anchor. In the autumn of 1720 Governor Rogers issued a proclamation that Rackham and his crew were pirates (not privateers) and therefore they were now on the wanted list of bounty hunters. A few weeks later, in November, Rackham and his crew – many of whom were drunk and unable to fight - were captured by pirate hunter Jonathan Barnet and his crew.

Rackham was taken back to Jamaica and hanged in Port Royal in mid-November and the two women were thrown in prison, sentenced to hang. Their executions were stayed because they were both pregnant. However, Mary Read died in April 1721, in prison, probably due to complications from the pregnancy. There is no evidence of Anne Bonny being hanged, and it is thought that she 'disappeared' somehow and made it to South Carolina where she died at the age of 85.

Local Trivia Question

Anne Bonny Crescent and Mary Read Crescent are two streets in Cayman. You have probably noticed them on your travels, but can you remember where they are?

Select the correct location from these choices.

a) They are near Camana Bay
b) They are off South Sound Road, near the Tennis Club
c) They are on Cayman Brac
d) They are in East End, near the library
e) They are in West Bay, near the Turtle Centre

answers on page 60

Pirate Timeline

Start at the bottom to follow the timeline of five contemporary pirates.

1782 Ann Bonny is thought to have died in 1782, aged 85, in Charleston, South Carolina.

1722 Anne Bonny was spared hanging while in prison because she was pregnant – then she disappeared. Black Bart Roberts was killed in action aged 39.

1721 Mary died from fever in a Jamaican prison, pregnant, aged 36.

1720 Mary Read joins 'Calico' Jack Rackham, fighting as a man. Anne Bonny (aged 23), and Mary Read were both captured with Rackham. Rackham hanged in Jamaica, aged 37.

1718 Anne Bonny was active with Jack Rackham. Blackbeard was killed in action, aged about 38.

1716 Blackbeard was active in the Caribbean.

1715 Mary Read moved to the West Indies.

1710 Anne Bonny was still only 13 or 14 years old.

1705 Rackham, Roberts and Blackbeard turn 18. Mary Read turns 15.

1697 Anne Bonny is born in Cork, Ireland.

1692 Earthquake, tsunami and subsequent disease kills over 4,000 people in Jamaica.

1686 One hundred years has passed since Drake landed in Cayman.

1685 Mary Read was born in England.

1682 Jack Rackham, Black Bart Roberts were born – possibly Blackbeard too.

Pirates in Cayman

We know that the explorer Columbus landed on the sister islands in 1503 and that Francis Drake the privateer made a stop in 1586 with a fleet of 23 ships. It seems that many ships, including pirate ships, found the islands a good place to visit because of their plentiful supply of meat. The islands had at different times been named after lizards, crocodiles, and turtles, which were abundant and would all make for a tasty addition to the diets of sailors.

The first temporary settlements were in Little Cayman and Cayman Brac, presumably, in part, because of their proximity to Cuba. There was a lot of pirate activity in and around Cuba during the golden age of piracy as it was an important base for the Spanish fleets carrying silver from South America. Cuba is less than 200 nautical miles from Little Cayman and Cayman Brac, and ships laden with silver often would have sailed through those waters, so it is very likely that pirates would have been familiar with the sister islands.

Blackbeard was probably familiar with Cayman too. In March 1718, Blackbeard and one accompanying ship sailed from Belize to the Bay of Honduras. There they added another ship and four sloops to their flotilla before sailing to Grand Cayman, where they captured a 'small turtler'. After Cayman, Blackbeard and his men sailed past Cuba and Florida on their way to Carolina. The infamous pirate should have stayed in the Caribbean. Blackbeard was killed in a fierce battle off Ocracoke Island, North Carolina later that year. He was shot five times and stabbed repeatedly in an attack led by Lieutenant Robert Maynard of the Royal Navy. After the battle Blackbeard's corpse was thrown overboard, and his bearded head was hung from the bowsprit of Maynard's sloop for all to see.

A survey of Cayman was carried out in 1773 by the Royal Navy and they found that the population was around 400, half of whom were slaves. It is likely that some of the landowners of the time would have been former privateers or pirates, or adventurers who had tried their luck - perhaps in Jamaica, Cuba, or some other large island, and had moved on.

Pirate Spot the Difference

Can you spot 15 differences between the two pirate pictures below?

solution on page 60

End of Chapter Pirate 'Test'

1. Who made the most money out of being a pirate?

   Blackbeard   Black Bart   Henry Avery

2. Who was the younger female pirate fighting alongside Rackham?

   Mary Read   Anne Bonny

3. Which pirate captured the most ships?

   Blackbeard   Black Bart   Henry Avery

4. Which pirate died of a fever in jail?

   Mary Read   Anne Bonny

5. Which pirate was shot in the neck?

   Blackbeard   Calico Jack   Black Bart

6. Which of these pirates lived to be 45 years old?

   Blackbeard   Black Bart   Calico Jack   None of them

7. Which of these were Calico Jack's flag?

   Skull and crossbones   Skull and crossed swords

   Devil-skeleton holding a spear

8. What was the name of Blackbeard's ship

   Royal Fortune   Queen Anne's Revenge   Golden Hinde

9. In which country was Calico Jack Rackham hanged?

   Cuba   The Bahamas   Cayman Islands   Jamaica

10. Which date below is within the *Golden Age* of piracy?

   1516   1617   1718   1819

answers on page 60

Pirate Movie Match-up

Match up the scrambled details of these famous pirate movies

Film Title	Star	Year
Treasure Island	Errol Flynn	2003
Captain Blood	Robin Williams	1991
Pirates of the Caribbean The Curse of the Black Pearl	Robert Newton	1995
The Crimson Pirate	Geena Davis	1950
Hook	Johnny Depp	1952
Cutthroat Island	Burt Lancaster	1935

answers on page 60

Answers for Chapter 4

Page 44 Morgan had 129 slaves

Page 47 Barbecue

Page 50 Kidnapped, The Strange Case of Dr Jekyll and Mr. Hyde

Page 54 Off South Sound Road

Page 57 Spot the difference

Page 58. 1. Henry Avery AKA Henry Every – operating in the Atlantic and Indian Oceans, so not well known in the Caribbean 2. Anne Bonny 3. Black Bart 4. Anne Bonny   5. Black Bart   6. None of them   7. Skull and crossed swords 8. Queen Anne's Revenge   9. Jamaica   10. 1718

Page 59. Treasure Island, Robert Newton - 1950
    Captain Blood, Errol Flynn – 1935
    Pirates of the Caribbean, Johnny Depp – 2003
    The Crimson Pirate, Burt Lancaster – 1952
    Hook, Robin Williams – 1991
    Cutthroat Island, Geena Davis - 1995

CHAPTER FIVE

Rum and Slavery

Rum

Rum may seem to be very much a Caribbean drink, but the fermented sugarcane concoction probably began in India or China. Marco Polo enjoyed a fermented 'very good wine of sugar' in the late 13th century in what is present-day Iran.

The first record of rum being distilled in the Caribbean is in Barbados in the 17th century. Molasses, a by-product of the sugar refining process, was fermented into alcohol by plantation slaves. Later, distillation was used to remove impurities and the world now had rum.

It may seem strange now, but rum was in such high demand in Colonial America that a rum distillery was set up in 1664, in what is now Staten Island, New York. Boston soon followed. Indeed, rum production became New England's most prosperous industry. In the 18th century, Rhode Island rum was an accepted currency, like gold, in Europe. Everyone wanted rum.

The bad part about the story of rum is that labourers were needed to work the sugar plantations in the Caribbean to support the demand, not only for the molasses to make rum, but also for sugar in Europe during the 17th and 18th centuries. A triangular trade was established between Africa, the Caribbean, and the colonies. Goods such as guns and brandy were exchanged in West and Central Africa for *people*, who were then shipped across to the colonies as slaves. The rum and sugar that these slaves produced was shipped across to England, where more exchangeable goods were gathered to trade for more slaves, and the triangle was repeated.

Slavery in the Caribbean

Unfortunately, there is a long history of slavery around the globe with stories of conquered people being used for sacrifice and labour since the dawn of so-called civilisation. This chapter deals only with slavery in the Caribbean after the colonizing superpowers settled in the New World. It is only part of the story, but hopefully shows some context and scale.

Hispaniola was the first centre of slavery, as it was the initial base for the Spanish. In Haiti, the first slaves were local Taíno Indians, who dwindled from a population of hundreds of thousands in 1492 to just 150 in 1550. As the indigenous population was dying of abuse and disease, African slaves were imported. The first 15,000 Africans arrived in 1517.

The Atlantic slave trade began in the very early 1500s. Santo Domingo (present-day Dominican Republic) was the first place to transport African slaves in the Americas. The deaths of indigenous people in the island caused the Spanish to quickly grant permission to import slaves from Africa to work the plantations.

France, another European powerhouse, took control of the western part of Hispaniola from the Spanish in 1697. In 1681 there had been 2,000 slaves there; by 1789 there were almost half a million.

In **Cuba,** the indigenous people were attacked and enslaved on a grand scale by the Spanish to work in the production of sugar cane. Sources say that Cuba's original local workforce was destroyed completely in the 1500s, mainly due to the lethal methods of forced labour on plantations. They were replaced, over time, by more than a million African slaves. After three hundred years of slavery there was a revolution by slaves in Haiti, resulting in the end of sugar plantations there. This meant that Cuba became even more profitable as the demand for its sugar increased. Even in the mid-19th century, when there was international pressure to abolish African slavery, Cuban plantation owners transported 100,000 Chinese workers to work there in extremely poor conditions.

Liquor

Liquors are all made by a process called fermentation in which sugars from an ingredient are converted into alcohol, which is separated from by-products of water and carbon dioxide. The catalyst in all this is yeast, which may be naturally present, as in the skins of fruit, or a cultivated yeast that is added. Grains are a typical basis of liquors and beer, meaning that most alcoholic drinks derive from a type of grass.

Some alcoholic drinks may have gone through a further process, called distillation. This is used to increase the ABV (alcohol by volume) level of the drink. Beer and wine are fermented but not distilled. Drinks like whisky and brandy are fermented and then distilled. Drinks that are distilled, the strong ones by volume, are what we know as liquors.

The typical ABV of each drink is shown in the table for comparing the relative strengths of each, but there can be a wide range of strengths within a category.

Drink	ABV	Base ingredient
Liquors		
Rum	40%	Grains - Molasses from sugar cane
Vodka	40%	Grains (corn, rye, others)
Bourbon	40%	Grain (rye, corn, wheat, barley)
Scotch whisky	40%	Grains - Malted barley
Brandy	40%	Grapes and other fruit
Grappa	35-60%	Grape seeds, stems, and stalks
Gin	40%	Grains (rye, barley, corn, wheat), traditionally flavoured with juniper berries
Non-liquors		
Beer	5%	Grains (barley, hops)
Cider	6%	Apples, pears
Wine	14%	Grapes
Champagne	13%	Grapes
Sake	18%	Grains (rice)

Fill in the blanks to match these popular brands with the spirit they sell.

1. Smirnoff	_____	7. Tanqueray	_____
2. Martell	_____	8. Beefeater	_____
3. Tanduay	_____	9. Mount Gay	_____
4. Grey Goose	_____	10. Maker's Mark	_____
5. Bacardi	_____	11. Glenfiddich	_____
6. Jack Daniels	_____	12. Old Havana Club	_____

The numbers in the table below are adapted from WHO (2010) data indicating the profiles of pure alcohol consumption by different countries (alcohol units, rather than volumes of liquid), given as percentages. Beer, wine, and spirits are self-explanatory whereas the 'Other' category refers to all other alcoholic beverages, such as rice wine, sake, mead, cider, and African beers such as banana beer.

The UK is given as an example – there they drink a broad selection of beer, wine, spirits and 'other' (probably cider). Drinking cultures change over time. Recently, for instance, wine has become Britain's favourite tipple showing the table to be a little out, but it is still good for broad comparisons.

Try match these six countries to the alcohol drinking profiles in the table.

USA Jamaica Russia South Korea Haiti France

Country	Beer	Wine	Spirits/Liquor	Other
	0.2	0.2	99.6	0
	42	5	51.4	1.6
	38	11	51	0
	50	17	33	0
	19	56	23	2
UK	37	34	22	7
	25	2	3	70

answers on page 76

The End of Slavery in the Caribbean

The French Revolution began in 1789, which had a massive knock-on effect on French territories around the world. In Saint Domingue (present-day **Haiti**) in August 1791, thousands of slaves began to revolt - killing and torturing their former masters. Slave rebels controlled one third of the island. The British and Spanish helped the rebels against the French rulers of Saint Domingue, for their own reasons of course, and so in a desperate move to keep the country French the government conceded to the slave rebels. As part of the bigger picture of liberty the parliament of the newly formed republic in France declared that all slaves in France and their colonies should be freed and should have French citizenship. This abolition was implemented after the Constitution of 1795 and all must have seemed like good news for black slaves in Saint Domingue, but it did not happen overnight.

For the next few years, The British tried in vain to conquer Saint Domingue. Their capacity to be victorious was hampered by tens of thousands of their men being killed by yellow fever caused by mosquitoes. All the while, the defence of the island was being led by General Toussaint Louverture. He was a former slave who had fought with the Spanish for a while to rid the island of the cruel, white, landowners and then changed sides to the French to push out the Spanish and make sure the British were unsuccessful in their attempt to gain control. Louverture emancipated around 40,000 slaves in Saint Domingue.

Portrait of Toussaint Louverture, 1813

From Alexandre Françoise Girardin - Anneaux de la Mémoire (Public domain).

Anneaux de la Mémoire (shades of memory) is a non-profit organisation dedicated to educating the world about slavery

In January 1801, Louverture invaded neighbouring **Santa Domingo** – the Spanish part of Hispaniola – and took it with little resistance. He promptly freed the slaves there too and declared himself Governor of the whole island of Hispaniola for life, but that would turn out to be shorter than he might have expected.

Napoleon Bonaparte sent 43,000 French troops to capture Louverture and retake Saint Domingue, which they did successfully, and Louverture died in a French prison in 1803. However, he had shown that freedom was possible, and later that year one of Louverture's generals, Jean-Jacques Dessalines, another former slave, led his revolutionary army to victory against the remaining French troops. On January 1st, 1804, Dessalines declared independence for the newly named Haiti, a Taino word meaning flower of high land, which was reluctantly recognized by France. Haiti became the first black republic in the world and only the second nation, after America, to gain independence from a European colonising power. The slaves had won.

However, on the Spanish side of Hispaniola slavery had not ended. There were battles and unrest for years until, in 1809, Spanish forces recovered Santa Domingo and re-established slavery there. Spain could not defend its territory from attack from the Haitians in 1822, who took control of both countries, and again abolished slavery. The Haitian leader of the now unified Hispaniola imposed a harsh life on the inhabitants of the Spanish side of the island, partly to help pay off debts to France, but slavery as such was over.

Unfortunately, slavery in the rest of the Caribbean and America continued, driven by the massive profits to be gained by not paying labourers. Eventually, right-minded individuals and organisations pressured their respective governments into changing their laws, and constitutions were re-written granting liberty as a fundamental human right.

When **America** won its independence from Great Britain in 1776, slavery was legal throughout the thirteen British colonies. Although not one of the Thirteen Colonies, **Vermont** declared its independence from Britain in 1777 and at the same time abolished slavery. Pennsylvania abolished slavery in 1780, and about half the states did the same either during the **American War of Independence** (1775-1783) or soon after. The federal government criminalized the international slave trade in 1808, but because of the industrial revolution in England and a huge demand in the 1830s for the new luxury item, cotton, a new wave of slavery began. Astonishingly, the value of slaves in America was seven times greater than the amount of currency in circulation in the country. Slavery, and anti-slavery, was at the core of the American Civil War. On January 1, 1863, President Abraham Lincoln announced the Emancipation Proclamation, making 3 million blacks legally free, and shortly after the Union won the war in 1865, the Thirteenth Amendment was ratified.

At the beginning of the 19th century there was no longer great profit to be made through the slave trade. Britain, who had been the world's largest slave dealers, passed the Slave Trade Act of 1807 – banning international slave trade, but not slavery. The Royal Navy even patrolled the African coast capturing 1,600 slave ships between 1808 and 1860. William Wilberforce had been working on the abolition of slavery since the French Revolution and his campaign was gaining momentum.

After the Haitian Revolution, Hispaniola no longer was a major player in sugar production, so whoever still used slave labour had an advantage. **Cuba**, who had been recently allowed by Spain to open their ports to foreign ships, became the world's leading sugar producers. They had the perfect climate, rolling hills and still had slavery. It was very difficult for British-ruled Jamaica to compete with Cuba, so from about 1823, the British Caribbean sugar industry went into a steep decline. There was little to be gained by the British government protecting the interests of the plantation owners. Also, in 1831, Britain heard of an uprising in Jamaica involving 60,000 slaves. The so-called Baptist War only lasted for eleven days but it sparked an inquiry that contributed to the end of slavery.

William Wilberforce

By Anton Hickel (1745–1798)

The anti-slavery campaign by Wilberforce in Britain was coming to a successful completion and the Slavery Abolition Act, 1833 was passed just three days before he died. The act abolished slavery in most of the British Empire, including of course, their islands in the West Indies. At first, only slaves under the age of six were freed, while anyone older was to serve out an apprenticeship for up to six years. The first so-called apprenticeships ended in 1838 and most of the rest finished in 1840. The British government had to borrow a substantial amount of money to compensate the slave owners, and the debt was not repaid in full until 2015.

After the Slavery Abolition Act over 800,000 slaves were freed in the **British Empire**. When full Emancipation occurred in **Jamaica** 311,000 slaves were freed. The entire population was only around 371,000 at that time. Similarly, slavery was abolished in the **Cayman Islands** in 1834. At the time of abolition, there were over 950 slaves owned by 116 Caymanian families.

Slavery, and trading in slaves, did not disappear overnight. **Puerto Rico** had been existing on a small-scale economy until it was given a boost by a Spanish Royal decree in 1815 which gave it much more freedom to trade. Plantation owners fleeing from countries like Haiti took refuge there, with slaves they had brought with them, so the island became more organized and profitable. The Anglo-Spanish Treaty 1817 made the importation of African slaves into Puerto Rico illegal, but the slave trade there continued – and even grew for decades. The vast majority of slaves were African, but they had not been recently transported across the Atlantic – they had been bought from neighbouring Caribbean islands. In 1812 there had been 12,000 slaves in Puerto Rico, but just thirty years later, in 1842, there were 41,000.

Abolitionists fought for many years to end slavery in Puerto Rico. Finally, on March 22, 1873, the Spanish National Assembly abolished slavery. Slave owners were compensated with 35 million pesetas per slave, and slaves were required to continue working for three more years.

A 19th century photograph of an enslaved Afro-Cuban

Amazingly, slavery continued in the region until the late 1880s – in the sugar plantations of **Cuba**. In 1820, a treaty between England and Spain had banned the importation of slaves from Africa, but in the following 10 years, 60,000 more slaves entered Cuba. In the late 1860s, Cuba began fighting the Ten Years' War for independence from the colonial powers, and slaves who had fought in that war were granted freedom in 1878. Finally, slavery and the indentured servitude called *patronato*, which was an obligation of a former slave to work for his master for no pay for eight years, came to an end by royal decree on October 7th, 1886. Cuba's period of slavery had lasted 373 years.

Spanish and French

The Caribbean has several French and Spanish speaking countries. Here are a few English words and phrases from Chapter Five. See if you can translate them into French and/or Spanish.

1. very good _____

2. sugar _____

3. only _____

4. first _____

5. three hundred _____

6. freedom _____

7. flower _____

8. black _____

9. The United States _____

10. small _____

11. money _____

12. countries _____

answers on page 76

The Price of Slaves

Slaves were a substantial investment, and their value was based on how much they could contribute to the wealth of their owners. A young, strong field-hand could be forced to work from dawn until dusk for decades.

St. John's College, Cambridge, shared documents from 1797 that included a list of the names, ages, and prices of slaves to be bought for English landowner William Perrin's sugar plantation in Jamaica. It is a catalogue of the 'valuation' of 35 men and 19 women, as well as children as young as 14, who had been valued for sale as slaves. The total amount came to £5,100 for the 54 adults, which the University of Cambridge estimated at £500,000 at 2016 prices. On average, that means that Perrin was paying £9,250 per slave, at 2016 prices.

This medallion is one version of an image used by abolitionists in the 18th century. Most famously, Josiah Wedgwood mass-produced it as a cameo for the The Society for Effecting the Abolition of the Slave Trade. High society ladies wore them in various forms, and the image decorated the clay pipes of gentlemen. Copies were hung on walls as works of art to help get the message across.

Am I Not a Man and a Brother - Josiah Wedgwood

True or False: The hymn, *Amazing Grace*, was written by the British politician and abolitionist, William Wilberforce. _____

answers on page 76

Famous Slaves

Here are five slaves from history; some of whom have been featured in Hollywood movies. Two would have been victims of the triangular slave trade, either directly or indirectly, and three are from further afield.

Fill in the blanks to complete the following biographical captions.

1. **<u>Aesop</u>** (c. 620-584 BCE) This man was a _____ (country) poet. His moral stories, or _____ usually had _____ as the main characters, such as The Hare and the _____.

2. _____ (c. 111-71 BCE) This Thracian served in the Roman army. He may have deserted before becoming enslaved. He became a famous _____ in Rome. He, and others of his profession, escaped and this famous combatant became one of the leaders in a major slave uprising.

3. _____ **<u>Khan</u>** (c. 1162 – August 18, 1227) He was the founder and first Great Khan (Emperor) of the M_____ Empire. He was enslaved in his teens but escaped and formed a formidable army. He was a ruthless leader and may have killed as much as 11% of the world's population in his conquests.

4. Hercules "Uncle Harkness" Posey (c.1748-1812) This African-American man served as the head chef for the Washington family, first at their forced-labor farm in Virginia and later, after _____ Washington was elected _____ of the newly formed USA, at their family home in the capital, _____. Posey escaped to New York and became a free man fifteen years later when Washington died. However, his children remained enslaved by Washington's widow, Martha.

5. Harriet Tubman (c.1820-1913) Harriet Tubman was born into slavery in Maryland, and started working from the age of five. She escaped to Pennsylvania in 1849, with the help of the 'underground _____ ', but soon returned to Maryland to help others escape. From then until the outbreak of the _____ War, despite having a bounty on her head, she undertook 13 perilous journeys leading a total of 70 slaves to freedom in Canada. She also provided crucial intelligence to the Union Army. It was announced in 2016 that Harriet Tubman would replace former President Jackson on the front of the _____ dollar bill, relegating the slave _____ to the reverse side. The banknote may be in circulation from about 2030.

answers on page 76

Black Lives Matter

A social movement emerged in 2013 in America, when a hashtag #BlackLivesMatter appeared on social media in response to the acquittal of a man who had shot dead a 17-year-old teenager. In 2020, between 15 million - 26 million people took to the streets of America in protest following the killing of George Floyd by Minneapolis police officer Derek Chauvin. There was global outrage against perceived racism and injustice and people in various countries began to think about how black lives mattered.

Citizens around the world began taking a hard look at the way their own neighbourhoods were still honouring doyens of the slave trade. Towns and cities, especially in the US and UK, had become prosperous on the backs of slavery in the cotton and sugar industries, and through the fundamental process of buying and selling people. A realization seemed to strike citizens that right before their eyes there were all manner of symbols of people who had been major players in the slave trade. Public buildings, statues, parks, and other venues all celebrated businessmen who had made their cities rich – at the expense of enslaved men, women, and children.

In the USA, many symbols of white supremacy and the Confederacy were removed, defaced, or destroyed - mainly across southern states. In the UK, the anger was more directed at the slave trade involving New World plantations. Protestors in Bristol tore down a statue of Edward Colston, a local 17th and 18th century businessman, philanthropist, and slave trader, and rolled it into Bristol Harbour. In January 2021, Oxford University dropped the name of Christopher Codrington from their library at All Souls College. Codrington, who died in 1710, bequeathed £10,000 to the library. A large part of his fortune came from his plantations in the West Indies.

On June 25, 2021, Derek Chauvin was found guilty of second-degree murder. How long was his prison sentence?

a) 9 years   b) 16.5 years   c) 22.5 years   d) 32 years

answers on page 76

Slavery Today

Exploiting fellow humans is not a thing of the past, nor is it related to skin colour. Unscrupulous people have been making slaves of less fortunate neighbours since 'civilisation' began. It was commonplace in ancient times for victorious tribes or nations to enslave the people they conquered. Nowadays slavery is more likely to take the form of human trafficking, and/or through scams in which a victim in dire circumstances in an impoverished or war-torn country may pay a sum of money to an agent who promises to set them up with highly paid employment elsewhere. The 'high pay' barely covers accommodation and transportation fees that the agent charges. The victims then become indebted to the agent and must work for years to pay him off.

The FIFA World Cup, hosted by Qatar in 2022, has been accused by many commentators to be an excellent example of modern slavery. Qatar did not have existing football stadiums or sufficient infrastructure to host such an event, so billions of dollars' worth of construction had to happen in a very short space of time. Poor workers from India, Pakistan, Nepal, Bangladesh and Kenya arrived in their thousands. They were housed in unsanitary squalor and had to work 12-hour days in searing temperatures. These migrants were subject to an Arab system of servitude, *kafala*, that gave them virtually no rights. Most took on debt to pay recruitment fees, signed away rights in contracts and handed over their passports to their sponsors. Some were not paid for months - but dare not complain for fear of being deported or imprisoned. Estimates of migrant deaths caused by the severe working and harsh living conditions in Qatar range from four thousand to seventeen thousand. The Qatari official estimate is in single digits.

FIFA World Cup question

One or two teams receive automatic entry to the world cup finals, without playing in qualifying matches. Why?

Answers for Chapter Five

Page 64

	Liquor/spirits	Suggested reason
Haiti	99.6	Lots of rum available
Jamaica	51.4	Lots of rum, but drink more beer than Russia
Russia	51	Lots of vodka
USA	33	Lots of beer, more whiskey, cocktails, and mixed drinks than wine
France	23	More wine, less liquor
UK	22	Wine, beer, vodka, gin, whisky
South Korea	3	Lots of rice wine and soju

Page 70.

1.très bon / muy bien (or muy bueno/ buena)

2. sucre / azúcar   3. seulement / solamente

4. premier (première) / primero / primera

5. trois cents /trescientos   6. liberté / libertad

7. fleur / flor   8. noir (noire) / negro (negra)

9. Les États Unis / Los Estados Unidos

10. petit (petite) / pequeño (pequeña)

11. l'argent or monnaie / dinero or la moneda

12. des pays / países

Page 71   False. It was written by John Newton, whose life was very interesting. Newton was pressed into service with the Royal Navy at a young age. After that, he was involved in the slave trade for decades, before, later in his life, he became involved in the abolitionist cause.

Page 72-73.   1. Greek, fables, animals, Tortoise   2. Spartacus, gladiator

3. Genghis, Mongol   4. George, President, Philadelphia

5. 'railroad', Civil, twenty, owner

Page 74   22.5 years

Page 75   They are the hosts and/or the holders of the trophy. Unusually, three countries will be hosting the 2026 World Cup. They will all automatically qualify.

CHAPTER SIX

Cayman Geography and Geology

The Waters of Cayman

You can find rivers in most countries, trickling or gushing downhill to the sea. Cayman does not have a river. The island is too small and flat and does not have any hills to speak of - so rivers do not form. Rain-water soaks into the ground or simply evaporates.

In most hilly islands the water that runs down the hills eventually goes into the sea, along with the silt that it has picked up on the way. This does not happen in Cayman – which is one of the reasons why the water around Cayman is so beautifully clear. So, why does the sea seem to have different colours?

Long, red wavelengths of light get filtered out at the sea's surface, so we see the sea as blue. Where the sea is deep, the blue is more intense. In shallower areas, Cayman's clear water allows the sunlight to go through to the bottom where it bounces back from a variety of sea floors as a much lighter blue colour. Phytoplankton and other microscopic phenomena scatter the light differently and give the water a greener or aquamarine appearance.

In some areas, the sea around Cayman has a beautiful turquoise appearance – but did you know these things about turquoise? Turquoise is a blue-green mineral that can be polished into a gemstone. It was named turquoise by the French, because it came to Europe from Persia, through *Turkey*. The Aztecs, indigenous people of the Mexico area, used turquoise to decorate masks, knives, and shields. In America, the Pueblo, Apache, and Navajo used it for amulets and jewellery.

How Deep is the Sea around Cayman?

The Cayman Islands rise from the seafloor of the Cayman Trough. Also known as the Cayman Trench or Bartlett Deep, this is the deepest part of the Caribbean Sea. It is over **25,000 feet deep**! That is deep enough to cover some very famous mountains.

The four mountains in the picture (facing page) are the highest in their respective countries. One is the highest in North America and one is the highest in the whole of the continent of Africa. Two are volcanoes. The last one's name does not begin with *Mount*. It is the highest peak in the UK and the British Isles, but it is not in England.

Name each mountain and the country that it is in.

Name	Country	Height
Mount _____	_____	20,310 ft (6,190m)
Mount _____	_____	19,308 ft (5,885m)
Mount _____	_____	12,389 ft (3,776m)
____ _____	_____	4,411 ft (1,345m)

answers on page 88

Mountains illustrating the depth of the water around Cayman

The Sister Islands

Grand Cayman is the largest of the three Cayman Islands, with an area of just under 76 square miles. Cayman Brac is much smaller, at roughly 14 square miles, while Little Cayman is even tinier - closer to 10 square miles.

The Bluff, from the south-east side of Cayman Brac

The Bluff on Cayman Brac is a limestone outcrop that rises gently from the western side of Cayman Brac to an impressive 141 feet (41 m) above sea level at the east. It is the highest point in the Cayman Islands. Brac is a Gaelic word for 'bluff', which means a small cliff, usually overlooking a body of water, or a plain where there once was water. Because of the porous nature of limestone, there are some interesting caves for exploring on the Brac. Diving and rock-climbing are also popular activities for visitors.

Take a guess:

a) In 2018, the population of Cayman Brac was (2,547   3,547   4,547).

b) The Brac is 12 miles long with an average width of (1.2   2.4   3.6) miles.

answers on page 88

Little Cayman

Little Cayman has around 250 residents, mainly expatriate workers and seasonal residents. The island has pretty beaches and world class dive sites. An estimated 20 Caymanians live there today.

Little Cayman

Christopher Columbus stumbled across the sister islands, Little Cayman and Cayman Brac, in 1503 - naming them *Las Tortugas* because of the abundance of turtles in the surrounding waters. In the 17th century, pirate ships and military vessels in need of supplies of fresh meat and water would call in to the sister islands to restock. Early settlers would provide ships with turtle meat, pigs and poultry, and fresh water from underground sources. However, one group of vicious, Spanish privateers in the 1670s prompted locals to abandon Little Cayman, leaving it unsettled until 1833.

The second set of inhabitants, probably members of Cromwell's army in Jamaica, settled in and around South Hole Sound at Blossom Village. At the beginning of the 20th century there were around 400 people on Little Cayman, but many families moved to Cayman Brac after the hurricane of 1932.

Bioluminescence

Cayman has a spectacular bioluminescent bay in which the water seems to glow in the dark. Bioluminescence comes from biochemical reactions in living organisms producing energy, which is given off as light. One bay in Cayman has very high concentrations of these bioluminescent phytoplankton.

Marine creatures rely on bioluminescence for communication, attraction and for finding or stunning prey. It can also be used for camouflage or to confuse predators. It is estimated that about three out of every four sea creatures are either bioluminescent or host bacteria that have similar effects.

Bioluminescent Organisms (Land and Sea)

ANAGRAMS

riffley   _____   outscop   _____

sheflaring   _____   unfig   _____

flishylej   _____   uqsdi   _____

growlmow   _____ _____

answers on page 88

Cayman's Coastline

Cayman is known for its beautiful, white, sandy beaches and Seven-Mile Beach is often voted among the top ten beaches of the world. Its sand is formed by erosion and the excreted calcium of parrotfish. Not all of Cayman's coastline is sand though. Here are some other geological terms relating to Cayman.

Ironshore   Ironshore is an unusual black-covered and jagged limestone formation. The weird flame-like pinnacles and ridges are caused by algae, boring through and dissolving the relatively soft rock. Ironshore is most often found at the coast, but the most famous place to find it is at Hell, West Bay, behind the Post Office.

Dolostone   This is a sedimentary carbonate rock similar to limestone, but containing the mineral dolomite, which is made up of magnesium and calcium.

Caymanite Caymanite is a semi-precious gemstone that is found in areas of the islands that formed in the Miocene (about 23 million to 5 million years ago). It is used in jewellery, and the different strata of colours look stunning when polished. It was formed from sediment that filled gaps between the limestone, and its different layers of colours are due to the metal mineral content of the sediment. The browns and reds are from iron, blues and greens from copper and greys from manganese.

Contrary to information that can be found on the internet, Caymanite was not formed by volcanic eruptions – obviously, Cayman never had volcanoes. It is commonly believed that it can only be found in Cayman, but that is not quite correct. Versions of it have been found in Hungary and Australia, but they are not silicified or laminated sufficiently to be turned into gemstones. Cayman has the best.

North, South, East and West

If you think you know where Cayman is in relation to other places, try this test. Imagine that you sail in a straight line from Grand Cayman along the 4 main compass points. **Where would be the first place you would land?**

Choose from the 3 options.

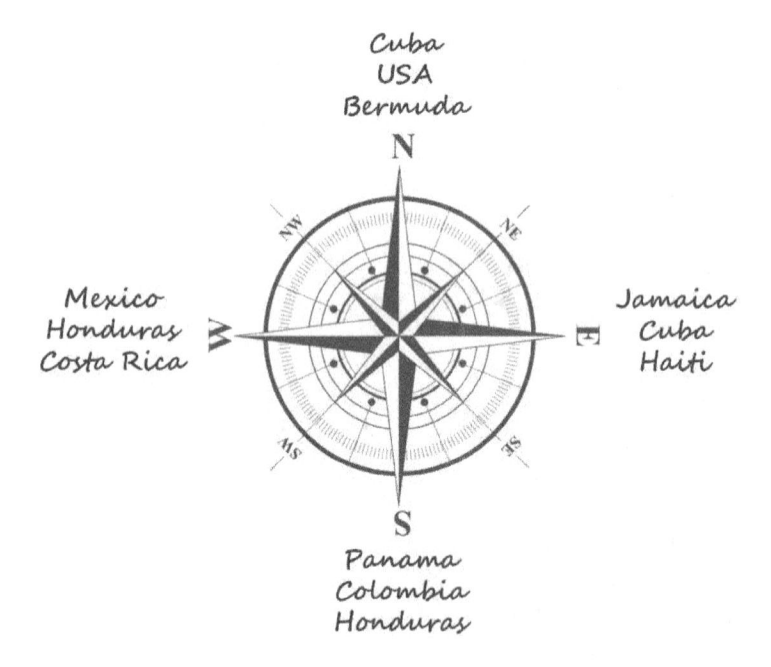

Cuba
USA
Bermuda

N

Mexico
Honduras
Costa Rica

Jamaica
Cuba
Haiti

S

Panama
Colombia
Honduras

answers on page 88

Cayman Roads

Here are the names of 21 of Cayman's most travelled roads and streets.

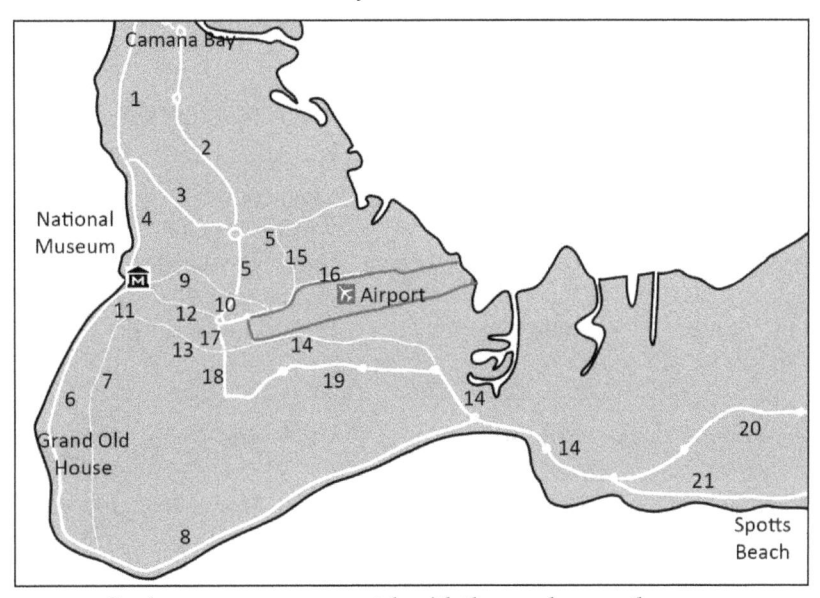

See how many you can match with the numbers on the map.

South Sound Road, North Sound Road, West Bay Road, East-West Arterial Road, South Church Street, North Church Street, Eastern Avenue, Esterly-Tibbetts Highway, Linford Pierson Highway, Bobby Thompson Way, Thomas Russell Avenue, Shamrock Road, Crewe Road, Boilers Road, Shedden Road, Walkers Road, Smith Road, Roberts Drive, Dorcy Drive, Huldah Avenue, Elgin Avenue

1.	8.	15.
2.	9.	16.
3.	10.	16.
4.	11.	18.
5.	12.	19.
6.	13.	20
7.	14.	21.

answers on page 88

Dive Sites

Perhaps you know the waters around Cayman better than the roads. That would be understandable considering the number of world class dive sites there are in Cayman's crystal-clear waters.

Try to match each of the dive sites listed below with its general location

Cinderella's Castle	Wreck of the Balboa	Lemon Wall
Armchair Reef	Bullwinkle's Reef	Grouper Grotto
Devil's Grotto	Rusty's Caves	Wreck of the Cali
Trinity Caves	Disappearing Canyon	Wreck of the Oro Verde
Eagle Ray Pass	Doc Poulson	Hammerhead Hill
Blue Pinnacles	Hole in the Wall	Oriental Gardens

North-west Point to Smith Cove   North Coast

GRAND CAYMAN

Smith Cove to Bodden Town

Bodden Town to East End

answers on page 88

Sand Colours

As mentioned elsewhere in this book, sand in Cayman is white – coming from calcified green algae deposited by parrotfish and sea urchins and by other matter such as crushed shells - eroded into fine particles by wave action and bleached by the sun.

Other beaches around the world vary in colour. Here are a few, with brief explanations and examples of where they might be found.

Orange: Volcanic and/or unusual orange limestone. Malta, Sardinia.

Black: Dark minerals on top of silica, near volcanoes. Tahiti, California, Hawaii, Greece, Dominican Republic.

Purple: Manganese deposits. California.

Red: High iron content. Hawaii, Galapagos Islands, Santorini (Greece)

Chocolate brown: Bluish-grey limestone mixed with volcanic greenstone. California.

Pink (rare): Near large coral reefs with creatures that leave red skeletons. Bahamas, Puerto Rico, Bermuda, Barbados.

Green (rare): High in olivine crystals from basalt lava flows. Hawaii, Guam, Galapagos Islands.

Answers for Chapter 6

Page 78:

Mount Denali – formerly Mt. McKinley (USA)   Mount Kilimanjaro (Tanzania)

Mount Fuji (Japan)   Ben Nevis (Scotland)

Page 80:   Population 2,547, 1.2 miles wide

Page 82: firefly, octopus, anglerfish, fungi, jellyfish, squid, glowworm

Page 84: North – Cuba, West – Mexico, East – Haiti (you would miss Jamaica),

South - Panama (or if you set off from the western side/ George Town area of Grand Cayman you might hit the tiny Colombian island of Providencia

Page 85: Roads and Streets

1.West Bay Road	8. South Sound Road	15. Dorcy Drive
2. Esterly-Tibbetts Highway	9. Shedden Road	16. Roberts Drive
3. Eastern Avenue	10. Thomas Russell Avenue	17. Huldah Avenue
4. North Church Street	11. Boilers Road	18. Bobby Thompson Way
5. North Sound Road	12. Elgin Avenue	19. Linford-Pierson Highway
6. South Church Street	13. Smith Road	20. East-West Arterial Road
7. Walkers Road	14. Crewe Road	21. Shamrock Road

Page 86: N-W Point to Smith Cove: Devil's Grotto, Trinity Caves, Wreck of the Balboa, Doc Poulson, Wreck of the Cali, Wreck of the Oro Verde

Smith Cove to Bodden Town: Armchair Reef, Bullwinkle's Reef, Oriental Gardens

North Coast: Cinderella's Castle, Eagle Ray Pass, Blue Pinnacles, Hole in the Wall, lemon Wall, Hammerhead Hill

Bodden Town to East End: Rusty's Caves, Grouper Grotto, Disappearing Canyon

CHAPTER SEVEN

Under the Sea

Spot the Animal

This picture contains some of the oldest members of the animal kingdom, all of which can be found in Cayman waters.

Simply answer Yes or No to the question, **"Is this an animal?"**

Eel	Yes/No
Fish	Yes/No
Sponge	Yes/No
Octopus	Yes/No
Sea Fan	Yes/No
Coral	Yes/No
Starfish	Yes/No
Sea Urchin	Yes/No

answers on page 111

Marine Life Word Search

Find the 20 names of sea creatures hidden in the grid.

Most are fish - but if they have the suffix 'fish' it has been removed.

N	A	R	M	R	T	U	R	T	L	E	O	R	T
O	C	T	O	P	U	S	A	L	T	R	D	R	R
D	A	M	S	E	L	N	D	I	E	R	O	A	I
R	T	A	R	P	O	N	A	O	T	C	R	W	G
T	A	A	G	S	T	M	E	N	K	U	E	R	G
S	M	E	E	B	A	R	Q	B	O	G	P	A	E
Q	E	A	F	O	N	P	E	G	I	S	P	S	R
U	S	A	N	X	G	A	A	E	G	M	A	S	A
I	R	T	M	T	U	G	A	S	A	U	N	E	N
R	O	O	L	T	A	H	P	H	O	G	S	L	G
R	H	O	Y	R	O	L	F	I	L	E	I	I	E
E	A	A	E	A	G	L	E	R	A	Y	D	L	L
L	E	U	L	T	A	R	T	E	L	M	A	H	E
Y	S	A	M	O	R	A	Y	E	E	L	O	E	P

Words to Find

ROCK BEAUTY	SQUIRREL	SNAPPER	LION
EAGLE RAY	TARPON	SEAHORSE	TANG
MORAY EEL	MANTA	HAMLET	BOX
TRIGGER	WRASSE	OCTOPUS	ANGEL
DAMSEL	TURTLE	HOG	FILE

Solution on page 111

Stingray Facts

The largest, sea-dwelling stingray in the world is the short-tailed stingray. It can be found in the sea near South Africa, Australia, and New Zealand. It grows to about 7 feet across and can weigh 770 pounds (350kg). Southern stingrays like the ones at Stingray City, Cayman, tend to be smaller than 5 feet across and weigh about 160 pounds.

Stingray venom is very painful, but usually not deadly, though it can cause cell damage and affected parts might need amputation if not treated promptly. Deaths are uncommon because most injuries are to the legs of swimmers or divers, not near vital organs. However, the barb itself is like a knife. 'Crocodile Hunter' Steve Irwin died from a stab to the heart by an Australian Bull Ray's 8-inch sting.

Southern Stingray, like the ones at Stingray City

Which of the following can a stingray use to detect prey?

a) The sense of smell   b) The sense of hearing   c) The sense of sight

d) They can detect electric fields   e) They can detect tiny vibrations

answer on page 111

Manta Rays

According to Guinness World Records, the largest member of the ray family is the Atlantic manta ray, which has an average wingspan of 5.2–6.8 m (17–22 ft). The largest manta ray wingspan ever recorded is 9.1 m (30 ft). To help you visualise how big that is, here is a truck pulling a 30-foot trailer!

The word *manta* comes from the Spanish word for:

a) massive   b) blanket   c) devil

answer on page 111

Sea Stars or Starfish

Here are 8 statements about starfish, but one statement is NOT true.

Can you detect the false statement?

1. Starfish have no brain.
2. Starfish have no blood.
3. Starfish usually have 5 arms, but some have more (one starfish has 24 arms and is 40 inches across).
4. The scientific name for starfish is Asteroida.
5. Starfish are fish.
6. If one of their limbs gets bitten off, starfish can grow one back in about a year.
7. When they capture prey, they keep hold of it with suction cups. Then their stomach exits their mouth to digest the food and re-enters the body when they have finished eating.
8. Some starfish can see in the dark, at depths of almost 1km, with eyes that are at the ends of their arms.

If you visit Starfish Point in Cayman, please keep the starfish under the water. If you see anyone lifting them out of the sea, please tell them to put them back in straight away before they drown. Starfish can die very quickly out of water and can even die from the stress of being handled under water.

answer on page 111

Hermit Crabs

Most animals are symmetrical, but hermit crabs are among those that are not. Hermit crabs have 5 pairs of legs. The first pair of legs has claws, and one is much bigger than the other.

When her eggs are due to hatch, a pregnant female hermit crab will go to the sea and scrape the eggs from her appendages. The tiny zoea will spend some a few weeks in the water growing. They need to grow antennae and more legs and claws before they can leave the water. Eventually, if they don't get eaten by fish, they make their way to the beach and find a shell to slip into. Hermit crabs have a soft and vulnerable abdomen, so shells provide protection from the hot sun and predators.

As they grow, hermit crabs need larger shells. Sometimes they may be lucky on their travels and find an empty one. On other occasions, as they tend to live in large groups, they organise themselves to do a coordinated trade-up. A BBC nature programme showed a gathering in which several crabs arranged themselves in size order, slipped out of their shells at the same time, and climbed into the bigger shells of their neighbours.

Seahorses

A seahorse propels itself vertically by fanning a small fin on its back – using tiny fins near the back of its head for steering. Seahorses have no teeth or stomach. They do not digest food like we do, so they must eat plankton all day long. Seahorses are masters of disguise. They are perfectly camouflaged amongst the coral.

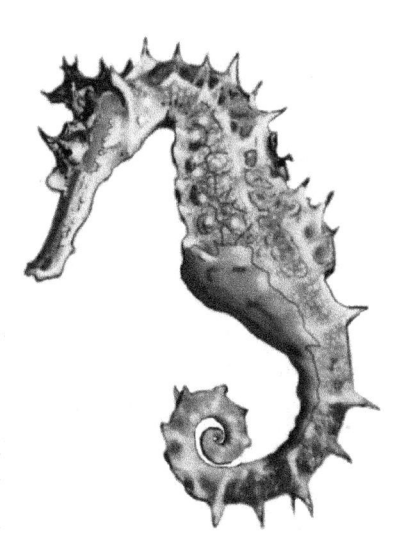

Seahorse comes from a Greek word, hippocampus. *Hippo* is Greek for horse, and the *campus* part comes either from the word for monster or caterpillar. They must have some scary caterpillars in Greece! There are other Greek names that we use for animals. Ever heard of a hippopotamus? This quite fancy name means 'river horse' in Greek.

Highlight your choice of answer for each of these sentences

1. Seahorses prefer to swim (**alone/ in pairs with their tails linked).**

2. When they mate, the **(male/female)** gets pregnant and carries the eggs.

3. Seahorses (**lay eggs in the coral/ give birth to tiny, fully formed seahorses**).

4. The dwarf seahorse is the **(slowest/fastest)** swimming fish in the world.

5. When a male wants to impress a female, he does a courtship dance that lasts for **(3 hours/ 8 hours).**

answers on page 111

Conch (pronounced "konk")

One of the most beautiful, and largest seashells that can be found anywhere in the world belongs to the queen conch. These marine molluscs produce a strong shell that is between 6 -12 inches long.

Female conch lay eggs in shallow water, where the sea has a sandy bottom. One individual can lay up to 10 million eggs in a single spawning season. Eggs hatch after four days and the planktonic larvae (known as veligers) drift with the current for between 14 to 60 days. After reaching lengths of about a half-inch, they sink to the sea bottom and hide. There they morph into juvenile forms and grow to about a 4-inch length. Finally, they move into nearby seagrass beds, where they form groups and stay until sexually mature. That happens at about 3.5 years of age when they reach their maximum adult length. By this time, their outer lips are at least 0.3–0.4 inches thick. Conch can live to be about thirty years old.

Sea water contains many minerals, including calcium. Conchs make their shell, like most molluscs do, by secreting a calcium carbonate gel that becomes hard when it comes in contact with water. Conch shells are heavy, with a spiny outer layer and a very pretty, pink inner lip that makes them very desirable as ornaments.

Marinated conch, conch stew, conch chowder and conch fritters are popular delicacies in the Caribbean. Being such a popular food can be unhealthy for an animal and many countries set limits to how many conchs may be taken from the water in one day and set aside marine parks where conch and other species must be left untouched. Without these restrictions, species can easily be overfished - which means that future generations will not have any conch.

Because conchs live in shallow water, fishermen can swim down and catch them by hand. You may have found a discarded conch shell on the beach and wondered why it had a hole in it. This is where the fisherman has cracked it, so that he can scrape inside and detach the muscle that is used by the animal to anchor itself to the shell. Amazingly, nurse sharks can produce enough pressure to suck a conch right out of its shell.

A conch and other shells, from a pastel painting by John Clark

True or False:

1. Conchs eat small fish _____

2. Conchs are snails _____

3. The queen conch produces pearls _____

4. Conchs are eaten by some species of turtles, sharks, and rays _____

5. Conchs eat algae and marine plants _____

6. Conchs are good swimmers _____

answers on page 111

Turtles

Green turtles, loggerheads and hawksbills can all be seen in the waters around Cayman. A turtle is sufficiently important to Cayman to warrant a place on the nation's flag. Also, the Department of Tourism holds the trademark for the pirate turtle, 'Sir Turtle' – most often associated with the island's national carrier, Cayman Airways.

The turtle that you are most likely to see while swimming is a green turtle, which seems to be misnamed, as it has a beautiful brown shell and a cream belly. The 'green' part of their name comes from the colour of their fat, which is probably affected by their diet of seaweed, algae, and seagrass.

Turtles are graceful swimmers and can quickly accelerate away from snorkelers and divers if they wish, and the distances they can swim are extraordinary. One green turtle in the Indian Ocean, being tracked by satellite, swam 4,000 miles without stopping for food. Most will routinely travel 1,500 miles between their feeding grounds and the beach from where they hatched.

The largest turtle ever recorded was a ten-foot-long leatherback, weighing 2,019 pounds (916kg) - which is about the same as a fully grown, male American bison. The prehistoric turtle, Archelon, lived about 75 million years ago and was about 15 feet in length. Its front flippers were each about the same length as a man.

Turtles have a similar lifespan to humans. Tortoises are also classified as turtles, and these land-dwellers have been known to live for over 150 years. The most obvious difference between the two is that tortoises have 'feet' and turtles have flippers. Also, turtles are omnivorous, whereas tortoises are vegetarians.

A good place for snorkelers to see green turtles like this one is
in the sea off Spotts Beach, on Grand Cayman's south coast.

**Try these questions on the Cayman Turtle Centre, Cayman's top
land-based attraction.**

a) The Cayman Turtle Centre dates back to …   **1968 1975 1981**

b) Construction on the present site and water park began in the same
year as Hurricane Ivan struck.   **True/ False**

c) The Turtle Centre also has an aviary. **True/False**

answers on page 111

Reef Fish

Question: What do a parrot, a squirrel, a lion, and an angel have in common?

Answer: You can put the word *fish* on the end of each to make a name of a tropical fish.

Have a look at the picture on the facing page.

1. Identify each species of fish.

Parrotfish, French angelfish, squirrelfish, and lionfish are there.

2. What is the fifth one in the picture?

Clue: It also ends with ……………. *fish*.

3: One of them is unpopular because it is an *invasive species*. Which one?

answers on page 111

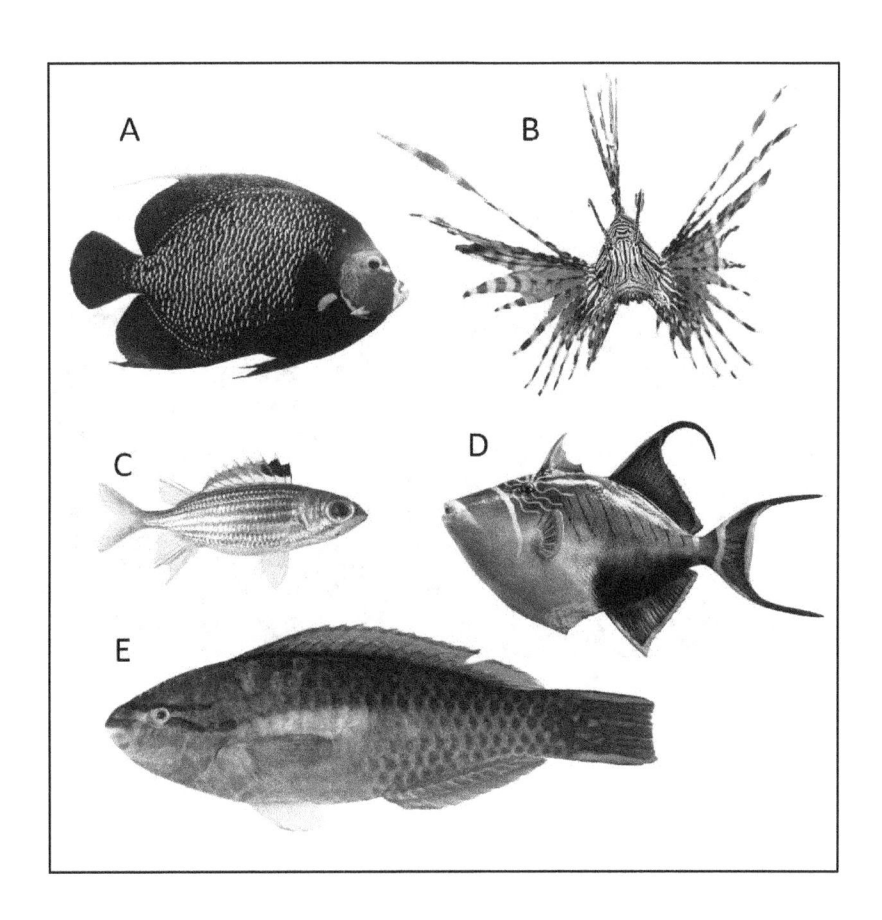

Sharks

Sharks have been around even longer than stingrays. Ancient sharks were swimming around the islands **450** million years ago – over 200 million years before dinosaurs – even before insects and trees!

Modern sharks have been terrorizing the waters for 100 million years.

True or False?

1. A shark can produce between 20,000 and 40,000 teeth in its lifetime.

2. Shark rib bones are twice as strong as those of humans.

3. Sharks can detect electromagnetic fields – which helps them find prey.

4. Sharks need bright light to see - so they cannot hunt at night.

5. The great white shark is the fiercest predator in the sea.

6. Hammerhead sharks never swim in Cayman water.

answers on page 111

The Coral Reef

Charles Darwin was one of the first people to become an expert on coral reefs. Before he published his famous book, *On the Origin of Species by Means of Natural Selection*, he had already classified coral reefs into three distinct types and arrived at an explanation of how coral atolls are formed.

The type of reef that is typical of Caribbean islands, such as Cayman, is a fringing reef. Fringing reefs grow near the coastline around islands and continents. They are separated from the shore by narrow, shallow lagoons and often run parallel with the shore.

Reefs are teeming with life – not just fish, lobster, crabs, octopus, and other animals – the coral itself is alive. There are soft corals like the sea pen and the sea fan, and there are hard (stony) corals like elkhorn or brain corals. Much of the stony coral is calcium carbonate, secreted by the soft polyp to form a hard, protective skeleton. The soft coral polyps grow on top of the hardened limestone. Some of the sand on beaches is quartz that has eroded from rock over thousands or millions of years. Much of the white sand of Cayman's beaches is recycled hard coral. Parrotfish bite and scrape away at the coral with their parrot-like beaks for nutrients found in the algae that lives on it. The calcium-carbonate reef material is not digested. It is ground up and excreted as fine sand which eventually washes up as a white, sandy beach.

Humans - Scuba Divers

SCUBA is what is known as an acronym. Most people in Cayman are very familiar with diving and are likely to know what the letters stand for. Do you? Some of the letters are provided here to help.

S _ _ _   C _ n _ _ _ _ _ _   U _ _ _ _ w _ _ _ _

B _ _ _ _ _ _ n g   A p _ _ _ _ _ _

Many would say that there is a specific feature that acronyms should have. This feature is present in four of these abbreviations. Which one does not have the feature and is therefore the odd one out?

NASA   NATO   FBI   AIDS   PADI

Try to arrange these diving related historical milestones in the correct order.

1864	
1910	
1933	
1943	
1960s	
Late 1980s	
Mid 1990s	

A. Dive computers become more widely used and trusted.

B. Adjustable buoyancy life jackets become available.

C. First pressure regulator invented (though it still needed a surface supply).

D. Semi-closed circuit rebreathers become available for the recreational scuba market.

E. Full face mask replaced goggles, nose-clip and valve.

F. The *Davis Submerged Escape Apparatus* was invented. A rebreather initially designed for submarine crews.

G. Jacques Cousteau registered the *aqua-lung,* now commonly referred to as a diving regulator or demand valve.

answers on page 112

Atmosphere: Scuba Diving

There is air pressure pushing against us all day long. From the top of the sky down to the surface of the sea is one atmosphere of pressure (1 bar). If we swim down under the water the weight of the water is also pushing down on us. Amazingly, we only need to be 10 metres deep to experience one more atmosphere of pressure. At that depth, air will be compressed, and be twice as dense as it was at the surface. Consequently, the volume of air will now be half of what it used to be.

If we swim down 10 more metres, we will now have 3 bars of pressure above us – (one in the sky and two in the water). Air will now be pressed to one third of sea level volume and be three times as densely packed. At 40 metres, volume is one quarter what it was on the surface and at 50 metres, merely the length of an Olympic size pool standing on its end, the same amount of air is pressed into one fifth of its original volume (5 bar).

1. Why is it so critically important for divers to breathe in and out normally (not hold their breath) as they ascend?

a) So that the water pressure does not crush their bodies. Air pressure is strong, and our bodies are weak.

or b) Because the air that divers have in their lungs will expand as they ascend, even by a few feet, and could damage their lung tissue. Damaged air sacs in the lungs can leak and send air into places it does not belong – like arteries, where it can interfere with blood getting to the brain.

2. What is the recommended maximum ascent rate for divers, according to the US Navy Diving Manual (2016)?

a) No more than 30 feet per minute   b) No more than 60 feet per minute

c) The faster the better

answers on page 112

Humans – Free Diving for Sport

Humans have trained themselves to hold their breath and swim underwater for a minute or two, unencumbered by scuba gear. Some swim down to considerable depths - much deeper than scuba divers typically go. Some of the dangers that scuba divers face are not present in free diving, but the sport has some different dangers of its own, including a risk of shallow-water blackouts when resurfacing.

When it comes to breaking records in free diving, there are various disciplines, allowing for different equipment to be used for descent and ascent. These include combinations of being allowed to use weights, fins, dive lines and buoyancy devices. There are teams of support divers, stationed at specific depths and medics standing by in case of emergency. One expert diver, Audrey Mestre, died in 2002 trying to break the world record held by Tanya Streeter of the Cayman Islands. In this tragic case, there was a reported lack of support, including no doctor at the surface.

Records for free diving: (At the time of writing, 2021.)

Unaided (with only fins): Men: 129m (423 feet)   Women: 102m (335 feet)

No Limits: Men: 214m (702 feet)   Women: 160m (525 feet)

For comparison: The limit for recreational scuba diving (PADI, NAUI,) is 130 feet (40m). In technical diving, a dive deeper than 200 feet (60 m) is described as a deep dive.

Take a guess: For how long did Tanya Streeter hold her breath when she set her record - free diving to 525 feet?

a) 2 minutes   b) 2 minutes 52 seconds   c) 3 minutes 26 seconds

answers on page 112

Humans – Free Diving for a Living

In the Caribbean, free diving is a leisure pursuit, but on the other side of the world humans have trained themselves to swim down to considerable depths and stay there for a while, so that they can work!

The Bajan people of Malaysia fish underwater for up to five minutes at a time. They are born and live on houseboats. Going ashore is so rare that many Bajans report being 'landsick' whenever they step onto the mainland. Also, their eyes have adapted over generations and their underwater eyesight is now twice as strong as that of most people.

In Korea and Japan, the most famous freedivers are women. The Haenyeo women of Korea learned to fish for squid, octopus, abalone and seaweed from their mothers and grandmothers and can stay underwater for up to ten minutes. Japanese women, the Ama, are famous for collecting pearls. Most of them start as young girls and are still diving into their 70s and 80s. The way they exhale as they resurface produces a characteristic whistling noise.

You may appreciate how buoyant we are with lungs full of air. If the air in our lungs becomes compressed, or we exhale, we become less buoyant. Most people can start to sink after 15 feet or so as they become negatively buoyant. It is much easier to move around underwater when we are in this state.

Three of the darkly shaded countries are where the world's most famous free-diving peoples live: Japan, South Korea, and Malaysia.

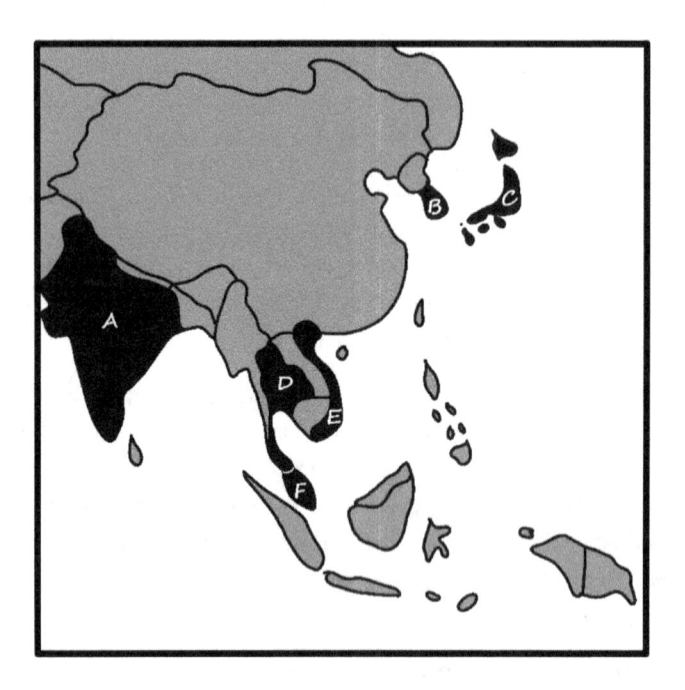

1. Can you identify them?

2. Can you identify the other three darkly shaded countries?

Choose from: The Philippines, India, China, Vietnam and Thailand

A. _____   D. _____

B. _____   E. _____

C. _____   F. _____

answers on page 112

Humans – Swimmers

Every year since 1985 the supreme swimming event in Grand Cayman has been a One Mile Sea Swim in the beautiful turquoise waters off 7-Mile Beach. That first event was sponsored by the Stafford family, and the next seven were sponsored by a George Town restaurant. It has been called the Flowers Sea Swim since 1993 and is the richest event of its kind in the world, based on the value of its spot prizes – with potentially one prize for every 7 swimmers.

Questions:

a) What was the George Town waterfront restaurant that sponsored the sea swim for 7 years?

b) It is called the 'Flowers' Sea Swim because it is named after:

- a shipwreck
- the bougainvillea along the beach
- a family that sells water

c) What was the total value of the prizes in 2019?

$10,000 $50,000 $100,000

d) Roughly how many swimmers enter the race?

500   750   1000

answers on page 112

Happy Birthday!

How many birthdays can creatures have in a lifetime?

The numbers below are not exact and are not the same for all animals in a species but provide a fair indication. Some kinds of shark live longer than other kinds of sharks; it is the same with most animals. Even a human life span can vary by about 25 years depending on where we live. In Chicago, people in the wealthy area live 30 years longer on average than those in the poorest area!

Use the table below to match up these Cayman critters with their average life expectancies.

Animal	Life Span
	5,000 years
	100 years
Human	82 years
	50 years
	35 years
	25 years
	12 years
Dog	11 years
	7 years

Turtle   **Conch**   **Shark**   **Sponge**

Iguana   **Spiny lobster**   **Starfish**

answers on page 112

Answers for Chapter 7.

Page 89. These are all animals, even the sponge and coral

N	A	R	M	R	T	U	R	T	L	E	O	R	T
O	C	T	O	P	U	S	A	L	T	R	D	R	R
D	A	M	S	E	L	N	D	I	E	R	O	A	I
R	T	A	R	P	O	N	A	O	T	C	R	W	G
T	A	A	G	S	T	M	E	N	K	U	E	R	G
S	M	E	E	B	A	R	Q	B	O	G	P	A	E
Q	E	A	F	O	N	P	E	G	I	S	P	S	R
U	S	A	N	X	G	A	A	E	G	M	A	S	A
I	R	T	M	T	U	G	A	S	A	U	N	E	N
R	O	O	L	T	A	H	P	H	O	G	S	L	G
R	H	O	Y	R	O	L	F	I	L	E	I	I	E
E	A	A	E	A	G	L	E	R	A	Y	D	L	L
L	E	U	L	T	A	R	T	E	L	M	A	H	E
Y	S	A	M	O	R	A	Y	E	E	L	O	E	P

Page 90. Wordsearch solution (left)

Page 91. All the senses mentioned

Page 92. blanket

Page 93. The false statement is 'Starfish are fish". They are echinoderms, like sea urchins. Everything else is true.

Page 95: 1. In pairs 2. The male   3. They give birth to fully formed seahorses 4. Slowest 5. 8 hours

Page 97: 1.false 2.true 3.true 4.true 5.true 6.false – but they can 'hop'

Page 99. a) 1968   b) True   c) True

Page 100: 1. (A) French angelfish, (B) Lionfish, (C) Squirrelfish, (D) Triggerfish, (E) Parrotfish

2. Triggerfish 3. The lionfish. **Lionfish** can cause damage, direct or indirect, to coral reefs, sea grasses and mangroves, due to their high rate of reproduction and growth, its voracious feeding capacity and lack of predators.

Page 102. 1. True   2. False. Sharks do not have bones. 3. True   4. False. Sharks can see very well in dark or night-time conditions. 5. False. Orcas win this prize. A hungry orca would even attack a great white. Orcas are also the fastest swimmers in the dolphin family. 6. False. Divers often see hammerhead sharks, but they are not aggressive toward humans.

Page 104. Self-Contained Underwater Breathing Apparatus

FBI. The others all make 'words' people can say. (Some would call FBI an initialism).

In order: C, F, E, G, B, A, D

Page 105. 1. 'b' To prevent damage when the air expands
2. 'a' 30 feet per minute. There should also be a safety stop 15 feet from the surface. Within 15 feet of the surface is where the greatest atmospheric change occurs.
Page 106: c) 3 minutes 26 seconds

Page 108. South Korea – B,   Japan - C,   Malaysia – F
Also: India – A, Thailand – D, Vietnam - E

Page 109: a) Lobster Pot b) a family that sells water   c) $100,000, making it the world's richest open-water swimming event   d) 1000 swimmers

Page 110. Sponge 5,000, Turtles 100, Spiny lobsters 50, Starfish 35, Sharks 25, Iguanas 12, Conch 7

CHAPTER EIGHT

Interesting Creatures

Mosquitoes

The female mosquito is a blood sucking marvel, using the blood of animals, including humans, as nutrients for her eggs. Her proboscis (the mouth part that she uses to stab us) contains six different 'stylets' - each having a specialised function. The mosquito's saliva is transferred to the host as she bites, and this can cause an itchy rash. Many species ingest pathogens while biting and transmit them to the next animal they bite. This is how they pass on so many killer diseases from one person to another. These include malaria, yellow fever, Zika, and dengue fever. Mosquitoes cause the deaths of over 700,000 people each year. Even humans, counting homicides and war fatalities in 'average' years, do not match such a high death toll.

The idyllic lifestyle of enjoying walks along the beach, relaxing in 5-star accommodation, and sipping cocktails by the pool is far removed from how Cayman was when mosquitoes ruled the island. The Mosquito Research & Control Unit was established in 1965 to prevent vector borne disease and to reduce the numbers of these bothersome creatures. Disinfection of visiting ships was implemented soon after, and the first 'mozzy plane' started spraying insecticide in 1971. As an indicator of the scale of the problem, in 1974 over 793,000 mosquitoes were caught in a single trap in Bodden Town. In 1996, small canals were made to increase water flow through the inland swamps. In 2003, larvicide became the main form of attack, and still is today. The battle against the mosquito has been a long, drawn-out affair, full of twists and turns. In 2016, Cayman experimented with releasing genetically modified male mosquitoes that would produce offspring unable to survive into adulthood. This method was never fully implemented but it shows the kind of lateral, scientific thinking that is necessary to combat such a worthy adversary while limiting damage to Cayman's ecosystems.

Overall, the efforts of the MRCU have been an outstanding success. Although mosquitoes may still be a nuisance for the short periods around dawn and dusk, they are bearably under control. Attractive as the idea might seem, we would not want to eradicate mosquitoes entirely because the males eat nectar and, in the process, pollinate all manner of plants. Mosquitoes are also an important food source for many other animals, including bats, birds, reptiles, amphibians, and even other insects.

The low-flying, MRCU 'mozzy plane' - in action

Mosquito question

A mosquito-borne virus caused a large outbreak of infection in Brazil in 2015. It was dangerous if contracted by pregnant women as it could cause deformities, including microcephaly, and dramatically increase the risk of pregnancy and childbirth complications? **What was it?**

answer on page 130

Iguanas

The blue iguana is endemic to the island and is an endangered species, protected by law. They are mainly land animals, with a diet of leaves, flowers, and fruit, though they may occasionally eat insects, fungi, and crabs. Adults do not have any natural predators so they can live long lives. One was known to have lived, in captivity, to the age of sixty-nine, which is virtually record-breaking for a lizard.

As Grand Cayman became more developed, the blue iguana lost its habitat and became critically endangered - on the verge of extinction. With the help of the CI Government, the Durrell Wildlife Conservation Trust, and other non-profit organisations, hundreds of captive-bred iguanas have been released into two reserves - the Queen Elizabeth II Botanic Park and the Salina Reserve. The Botanic Park has an education centre where people can learn all about the blue iguana - from egg to adult.

A Cayman blue iguana

The green iguana came to Cayman in the 1990s, though was rarely seen at first. It is an invasive species that causes damage to infrastructure, crops, and plants, and takes over the habitat of Cayman's blue iguana. They are arboreal and mostly herbivorous. The shiny metal collars that can be seen on tree trunks are to stop iguanas from climbing the trees. A shady spot under a tree would seem to be a cool place to park a car, but there is a risk, with iguanas around, that the driver could return to find a large mess of iguana poop messing up the windscreen and beginning to corrode the car's paintwork.

The numbers of green iguanas became a real problem from around 2014. They were everywhere, including shopping areas, car parks and schoolyards. It was difficult to drive for five minutes without seeing one squashed in the road. Between 2014 and 2018 the green iguana population rocketed five-fold from about 250,000 to over 1.3 million! A harvest management strategy was implemented, and a bounty was put on the heads of the pests. Over half a million were culled within a year by registered hunters, and by November 2020 1.25 million had been killed.

The iguanas had some respite for the 40 days that the 'shelter-in-place' order was in force for Covid-19, when no one was allowed to be out to shoot or catch them, but afterwards the Department of Environment soon resumed their management activities. It is now quite uncommon to see them – but there are still plenty of them around – deeper in the bush. The DOE is aware of how difficult it is to eradicate the green iguana, but they are on a mission to keep their numbers under control.

An invasive, green iguana

Iguana questions

1. Can iguanas swim? _____

2. What colour are adult green iguanas? _____

3. Do iguanas attack humans? _____

4. Are crocodiles more closely related to lizards or to birds?

answer on page 130

Scorpions

There are three types of scorpions in Cayman, including one that is unique to the island. Stings from scorpions can be very painful and the effects can last for 2-3 days, so it is best to avoid being stung - especially as scorpions can sting more than once in the same attack. Children, because of their smaller body-size, are more likely to be severely affected by a scorpion sting, potentially requiring hospitalisation. No deaths from scorpion stings have ever been recorded in Cayman, though death by anaphylaxis is possible for anyone unlucky enough to have a strong enough allergic reaction. People this vulnerable should probably be more fearful of bees, because of the chance of being stung by several at once.

Scorpions can climb walls, and come up drains, but a common place to find them would be in a shoe that has been kicked off and left outside – so check, carefully. They are nocturnal animals, usually and have been known to sting people as they lie sleeping, but creatures such as scorpions do not generally go looking for trouble, and they normally avoid humans. Accounts of people being stung are rare in Cayman. If you want to find a scorpion at night you could use an electric black light. The ultraviolet light makes them glow in the dark - as does moonlight.

"Bigger scorpions have stronger venom than smaller scorpions."

True or False?

Scorpion

answer on page 130

Centipedes

The most common centipede in Cayman is also one of the largest of the species; *Scolopendra morsitans*. Their first pair of walking legs adapted into venomous, 'poison claws' (forcipules) which help them capture insects, spiders, snails, amphibians and even small mammals! Centipedes are very, very old! They separated from other types of myriapods 460 million years ago – which makes them twice as old as dinosaurs.

These fast-moving centipedes are highly armoured, fast-moving and difficult to catch. Their segmented body is striped, and the head and tail are red or orange in colour. They inflict a painful sting, which, though not likely to be fatal, needs to be cleaned, as complications from infections can occur. Deaths from centipede stings are difficult to substantiate, but there may be one or two every ten years in the USA, compared with about 500 in the same period for deaths from bee and wasp stings. There have been no reports of severe cases in Cayman, and most people will probably not even encounter a centipede.

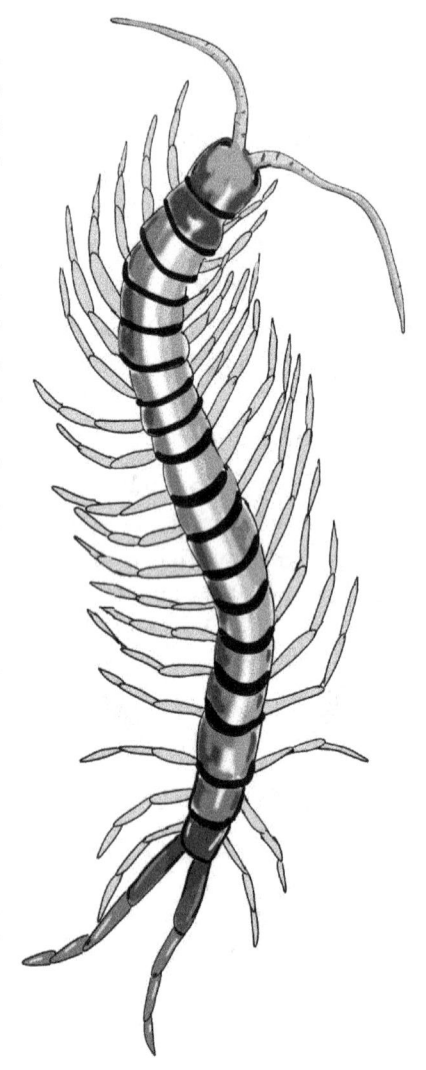

The average Cayman centipede is 13 cm long, so this sketch is roughly life-size.

50 spiders

There are around 50 types of spiders in Cayman, some more potentially painful than others. These are the main ones to avoid:

The brown recluse, or violin spider may give such a serious bite that it may require medical attention, but you would need to be very unlucky to be bitten. The spider is distinguished by a dark violin shape on its back. The fact that it is called a recluse gives a hint that you probably will never see one.

The brown widow spider is a cousin of the black widow. It also is a shy creature so poses little threat, and although its venom may be on a par with that of the black widow, the toxin seems to stay local to the bite, rather than circulating through the blood. Juvenile black widows are brown and look very similar to brown widows so it would be easy to get them confused – if you ever saw one.

The black widow spider lives in Cayman too! Drop for drop, its venom is 15 times more potent than a rattlesnake's. Fortunately, their preferred prey is a fly or a mosquito, not a 160-pound human, so they only deliver a relatively small dose of venom when they bite. Bites *can* be fatal, and small

children, the elderly, and those who are infirm are most at risk. However, fatalities are very rare. Even in the USA, where there are around 2,000 reports of bites from black widows per year, there have been no reported deaths since 1983.

Black widow spider

Cayman's huntsman spider is an impressive, large, hairy beast. Sometimes they are known as giant crab spiders or cane spiders, so that might indicate that they are easy to notice. Despite its size, a huntsman spider will probably want to run away if it sees you. On rare occasions they might bite, which would be painful, but not too harmful.

Last, but not least, Cayman is also home to tarantulas! These are hardly ever seen though and tend to live underground. Contrary to folklore and Hollywood, their venom is relatively weak, and tarantulas are only classed as a mild-bite hazard.

Which animal is most likely to bite and harm a human in Cayman?

a) centipede

b) barracuda

c) dog

d) spider

e) snake

answer on page 130

Land Crabs

There are four types of crab in Cayman, including the hermit crab. The blue land crab (Cardisoma guanhumi) is the biggest - and may be a different colour at different stages of its life, or whitish-grey if it is female. Its carapace (the big cover across its head/back) can be 6" across, and in males, its big claw can be as large as its carapace. The other front claw in males is smaller. These dinner-plate sized, ten-limbed creatures can appear in unusual places - such as half way up a mosquito screen on a ground floor window.

Land crabs live near the water, and like mangrove and swampy areas. They are well protected from predators by their claws, their nocturnal lifestyle and because they live in burrows a few feet deep. Their main predator is, as you might guess, humans.

Locals in Cayman hunt land crabs when the rainy season starts in June and July, when the crabs are migrating. They come out of their burrows in large numbers, at first to put on weight and do their courting and mating. Eggs are carried by the females for a couple of weeks but then need to be delivered to the sea. The spawning journey usually takes place within one or two days of a full moon, so it is easy to predict. Migrating crabs can be attracted to car headlights and flashlights, so that explains why you might be driving along in July and notice a couple of driverless cars, seemingly abandoned with their lights on. Be vigilant when driving in 'land crabbing season' because, apart from causing harm to a poor pregnant creature, driving over a sturdy mature crab can cause damage to your tyres or cause a driver to swerve. Environmentalists have grave concerns for the future of land crabs in Cayman.

Agoutis

Agoutis are large, South American rodents that are about the size of a rabbit and eat like squirrels. They are seen more often in eastern areas of Grand Cayman, but not on the sister islands. A good place to potentially spot one is the Botanic Park. Agoutis love to eat fruit or nuts that have dropped to the ground. Apparently, their teeth are so strong that they are the only animal that can crack open the hard outer shell of a Brazil nut. Agoutis live in burrows or hollows in tree trunks and pose no threat to humans. Though typically they would run away if they heard someone approach, they have powerful hind legs and can jump six feet straight up into the air if startled, so they could opt to use this as an escape manoeuvre!

Agoutis pair bond, which means that when they find a partner they stay with that partner for life. One to four babies are born in a litter and can run after just one hour.

Agouti also describes an animal's fur markings – indicating a two-toned patterning. Someone might refer to the fur of another animal, for example a cat, dog, or rabbit, with 'salt and pepper-effect' bands of fur, as *agouti*.

Agoutis are not indigenous to Cayman. They were introduced to help reduce the rat population a long time ago. Many countries have interfered with their own ecosystems to their cost – this one too, backfired. Rats are nocturnal, whereas agoutis come out during the day – so the two creatures seldom met. The agoutis did however eat Cayman's snakes, which had been keeping the rodent population down - so the rat situation got worse rather than better.

The Grand Cayman Parrot

Cayman's national bird is an iridescent green parrot with pink or red feathers around its throat, a white circle around its eyes and blue feathers in its wings that can be seen when it is flying. The Grand Cayman parrot, and the similar but smaller version found on Cayman Brac, are subspecies of the Cuban Amazon parrot. They are not found anywhere else in the world.

Amazon parrots, like the Grand Cayman parrot, eat fruit and seeds of indigenous plants. In Cayman they seem to favour red birch berries and sea grapes. They are most often seen in the morning or just before sunset, flying in pairs or family groups. Cayman's green parrots are often heard before they are seen and have a distinctive squawk.

Grand Cayman Parrot

Try these anagrams of other birds that may be found in the Cayman Islands

1. thick wild guns _____ _____

2. drape pins _____

3. bar ride gift _____

4. lunge or breathe _____ _____ _____

4. Can you identify this bird? _____

(It is easy to spot these on Cayman Brac.)

answer on page 130

Chickens

When looking through the animal kingdom for the closest match to Tyrannosaurus rex DNA, the nearest one is – the chicken.

Chickens have been domesticated for about 8,000 years. Which means that man was benefiting from their eggs and meat for two or three thousand years before even the first civilisation in Mesopotamia.

Chickens are everywhere in Cayman. It is common to see groups of these little dinosaurs in public places. Whether you are stepping off a luxury cruise liner or going to work in the heart of one of the world's major financial centres, you are likely to see (or hear) some of these farmyard creatures roaming free, without a care.

Here are 10 group nouns of animals you might find in and around Cayman. **See if you can match up the animals with their group names.** e.g. pride of lions.

pandemonium of ……..……   brood of ………..…………

army of …………………   shiver of ……..…….….

intrusion of …………………   flock of ………………….

fever of …………………   risk of …………………

lounge of …………..…………   cast of ………………..…..

Choose from: sharks frogs stingrays lizards crabs lobsters cockroaches chicks parrots chickens

answer on page 130

Cockroaches

Most people shudder at the mere thought of cockroaches, but these ancient insects deserve a considerable amount of respect. Today's cockroach is very similar to the one that was around 320 million years ago, in the swampy, Carboniferous period. We know that cockroaches can live happily in the sunny Caribbean and other hot places, but they also can be found in temperate and cooler places too, including the Arctic region. Some families of roaches can withstand temperatures of -122°C (-188°F) by making their own version of antifreeze. The cockroach most likely to be seen in Cayman is the rather large, American cockroach.

There are thousands of species of cockroach, but only a few are considered pests or pose a health risk to humans. Unfortunately, the ones found in Cayman are among these. They feed on human and pet food but need very little of it and may be inactive and unseen for long periods. They can go without food for up to a month. Cockroaches transport pathogens on their bodies, which is especially dangerous in hospitals, and are linked to allergic reactions in homes. Nearly half of homes with no signs of cockroaches show cockroach allergens in their dust.

The hardy creatures are showing signs of becoming resistant to insecticides, so other ways of dealing with them will need to be found. Folklore has it that cockroaches will inherit the Earth in the event of a nuclear apocalypse. Does this have any factual basis? Cockroaches can withstand radiation between 6 and 15 times stronger than doses needed to kill humans. Insects generally are less prone to negative effects of radiation. Indeed, scientists in Russia found that fruit flies exposed to some gamma radiation lived longer lives than those that did not.

Cockroach Quiz - True or False

a) A cockroach can live for up to one week without its head! T / F

b) American cockroaches live for about 1.5 years T / F

c) Cockroaches can hold their breath for up to 40 minutes. T / F

d) Cockroaches can run at over 40 body lengths per second. T / F

e) Most adult cockroaches have wings. T / F

f) Some species of cockroach can fly. T / F

g) Most cockroaches live in cities, in warm houses. T / F

answer on page 130

Cayman Animal Crossword   Clues

Across

3. When land crabs (and other animals) release their eggs and sperm in water **(8)**
6. Having an adverse reaction to something that does not affect most people (8)
8. Large hairy spider with a bad reputation (9)
10. Silk comes from spiders. What comes from sheep? (4)
13. You will find one on the end of a rat's leg or an iguana's, but not a spider's (4)
14 A bright source of light, important to mating land crabs (4)
15. Brownish spider as big as a hand (8)
17. A person who can follow an animal by its footprints and other clues (7)
18. Workers in Cayman do not pay this (3)
20. The sap and skin of this delicious fruit may cause irritation to some people
24. You might feel this way after being bitten by a black widow spider (4)
25. A crab that regularly upgrades to a bigger shell as it grows (6)
26. Cayman has two species of this bird; barn and short-eared (3)
28. Small vertebrates, like frogs, that need water or moisture to survive (10)
31. A reptile such as Cayman's iguana or gecko (6)
34. Term given to an animal that bites, stings, or propels its toxins (8)
35. Most lizards, snakes, rats, crabs, and billions of humans can do this in water (4)
36. One rotation of the Earth; most are sunny in Cayman (3)

Down

1. Long-tailed rodent pest (3)
2. Lethal (6)
3. Arachnid with pincers and a stinger (6)
4. Contrary to myth, you cannot get one of these skin lumps from toads (4)
5. A place where humans go to improve their strength (3)
7. The world's deadliest animal – translates from Spanish as 'little fly' (8)
9. Term that describes an animal that is active at night (9)
11. Small coastal tree or area of such trees – also a haven for wildlife (8)
12. Primitive, unwanted large insects that carry diseases and allergens (11)
13. Quick (4)
16. Poisonous (5)

Interesting Creatures

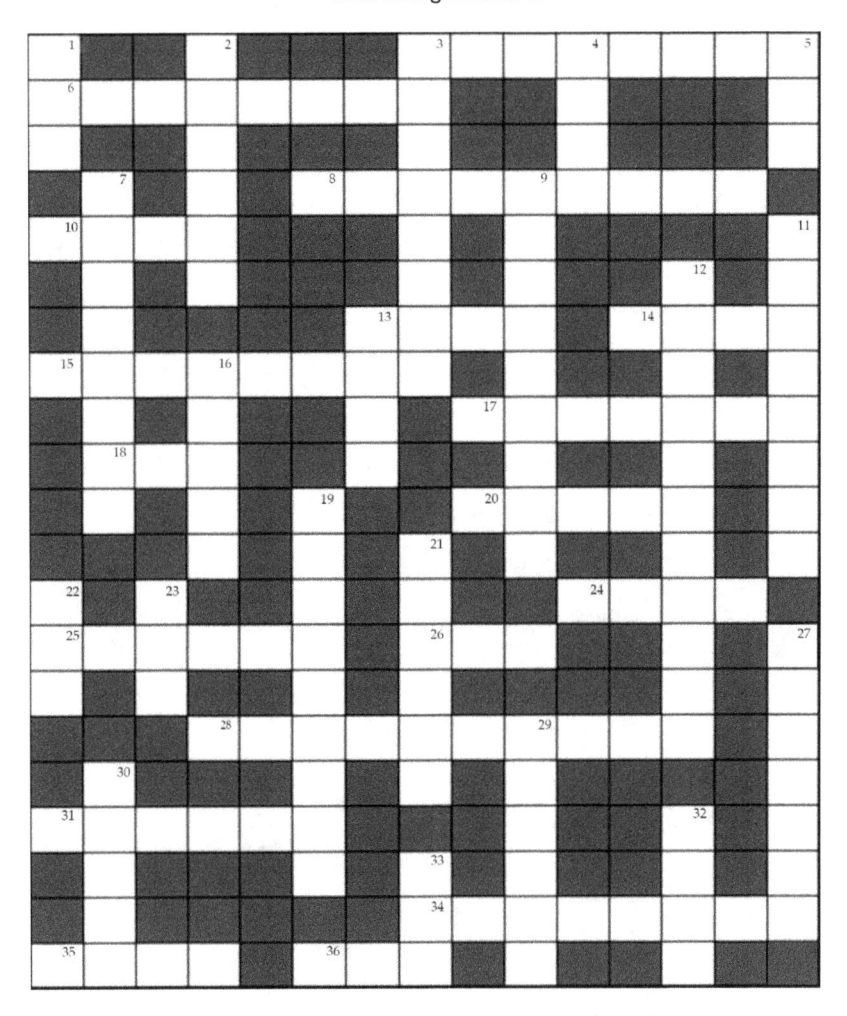

19. Long arthropod (cousin of the lobster) that eats cockroaches and termites (9)
21. Musical instrument marking on the back of a brown recluse spider (6)
22. Being nervous around people, like most Cayman spiders (3)
23. Small children might do this if bitten by a centipede (3)
27. Rabbit-sized, snake-eating rodents (7)
29. Large lizard. Cayman's unique blue one can weigh up to 30 lb (14 kg) (6)
30 A woman whose spouse has died (5)
32. An amphibian without a tail – capable of turning into a handsome prince! (4)
33. A creeping plant that can cause a nasty rash (3)

Solution on page 130

Answers from Chapter 8

Page 114   Zika virus

Page 116   1) Yes, they are very good swimmers. 2) Not green. Juveniles are very bright green, but adults are a rocky, stone colour. 3) Not usually. Although males usually grow to 1.7 metres long (5.6 feet), nose-to-tail, they are herbivores and, although they have been known to bite if attacked and injured, they do not pose much of a threat to humans. They will probably just scuttle away when they are approached. 4) Crocodiles are more closely related, phylogenetically, to birds than they are to lizards!

Page 117   False   Page 120   a dog

Page 124   Anagrams: 1) whistling duck 2) sandpiper 3) frigatebird

4) great blue heron   5) The bird in the picture is a booby

Page 125   pandemonium of parrots   brood of chicks   army of frogs shiver of sharks   intrusion of cockroaches   flock of chickens   fever of stingrays   risk of lobsters   lounge of lizards   cast of crabs

Page 127   All true except g - most live in the great outdoors

Page 128-129

CHAPTER NINE

Cayman History

Christopher Columbus sighted two of the Cayman Islands on May 10th, 1503. There were so many turtles swimming in the sea near these islands that he named the islands after the turtles.

What is the Spanish for turtles?

Las Tortugas   La Tortuga

Le Tartarughe   Las Caimanas

Twenty years later, on the Caribbean section of the Turin Map (c. 1523), the Cayman Islands had a different name – not related to turtles – **what was it?**

a) Los Mosquitos, meaning small flies

b) Los Lagartos, meaning alligators or large lizards

c) Los Cocos, meaning the coconuts

Since about 1526, the islands have been named after crocodiles! Caimans are freshwater alligators that live in Central and South America, usually in

lakes and rivers. The reptile after which Cayman is named is more likely to be an American crocodile or a Cuban crocodile. Both are salt-water animals.

answers on page 164

Discovery Day

Discovery Day is a public holiday enjoyed in the middle of May each year, to celebrate the anniversary of the day in 1503 that Christopher Columbus landed in the Cayman Islands.

Which two islands did he see?

a) Grand Cayman and Cayman Brac

b) Grand Cayman and Little Cayman

c) Cayman Brac and Little Cayman

answers on page 164

Cayman's First English Visitor

The first Englishman to step onto a Cayman beach was this man. In 1586, he and his 23 ships pulled up on the shores of Cayman and stayed for two days. He reported that there were no inhabitants, but numerous crocodiles, alligators, iguanas, and turtles.

Who was this intrepid explorer and seaman?

a) **Walter Raleigh**   b) **Francis Drake**

c) **Charles Darwin**   d) **Oliver Cromwell**

e) **William Shakespeare**

answers on page 164

1586

In the year 1586, when the first Englishman (from the previous page) stepped foot in Cayman, great things were happening, or about to happen in Europe. Here are the names of some very influential people of the time, and their ages in 1586. See if you can figure out who is who.

Francis Bacon was 25 years old in 1586.

Galileo Galilei and **William Shakespeare** were both 22.

Caravaggio was 15, and **William Harvey** was only 8 years old in that year.

Who is being described in the boxes below? Match them up.

1. This man revolutionised the field of medical science by mapping out the entire human circulatory system. Before him, no one had really known how blood was pumped through the body. He was a pioneer of physiology and anatomy.

2. This Italian was able to prove Copernicus' idea that the Sun (not the Earth) was at the centre of the solar system because he had made a telescope and had observed the movements of the planets.

3. This man helped science become scientific, advocating a methodological approach so that the investigators should not fool themselves.

4. This artist was still learning his art in 1586, and painted *Supper at Emmaus* (below) fourteen years later, in 1602. He was famous for his dramatic use of dark and light.

5. This man was possibly the best storyteller, poet and playwright of all time. His plots covered all of humanity's themes and will live forever. His plays include *Romeo and Juliet, Julius Caesar, Othello* and *Macbeth.*

answers on page 164

Tripadvisor c. 1599

Cayman appeared in what is described by scholars as a 'monumental' book, written at the end of the 16th century by Richard Hakluyt. It contained detailed accounts written by people who had experienced the New World first-hand, and the reference to Cayman was taken from the 1592 notations of Captain William King of the Saloman. This edition of the catchy-named tome, *The Principal Navigations, Voiages, Traffiques and Discoveries of the English Nation* even included a map using Mercator projections. Hakluyt mentioned the abundance of turtles around Cayman, and in his equivalent passage to a 'dining out' section of his guide, pointed out that two female turtles laden with eggs could feed 100 men for a day.

The First Ship built in Cayman - 1630

On Grand Cayman, from North-West Point, past 7-Mile Beach, down to Sand Cay, vessels have open access from the sea to the beaches, bays, and shoreline. The rest of the island is surrounded by coral reefs, which have been the downfall of many unfortunate ships. Scuba divers can probably reel off a list of shipwrecks they have swum through along Cayman's reefs. For seafarers who smashed their ships on the rocks in the 17th century, being shipwrecked was a disaster - and catching a flight home was not an option. The solution was either to stay, or in one case, rebuild!

In the early 1600s, although most of the area was owned by the Spanish, there were still many ships from countries such as England and Holland in this part of the Caribbean. Many regularly pulled into Cayman for turtles, which they would preserve with salt before continuing their voyages. In 1630, a Dutch ship called the Dolphin wrecked on one of Cayman's reefs. For the next 16 weeks their crew of 122 spent their days building a craft, which they named the Cayman. The yacht was sufficiently seaworthy to make the journey to Cuban waters, where they were rescued by Dutch ships.

Cromwell's Western Design

Oliver Cromwell

From 1654-1660 England and Spain were at war, so for years there was a culture of privateering and attacking each other's colonial possessions. In 1665, after the Anglo-Spanish War, but before any significant treaty was signed, Oliver Cromwell came up with a plan called the Western Design which included capturing wealthy Spanish assets in the Caribbean to add to Britain's colonial portfolio, the best of which was Hispaniola. Cromwell should have sent an elite fighting force to capture Hispaniola, but the troops he assembled were poorly trained, inexperienced, and very unlikely to succeed. Some of the men were from existing regiments of the army, but only the incompetent ones that their commanders wanted to release. To supplement the force, volunteers were needed, but the calibre of men who were recruited were malnourished refugees who had left their own poverty-stricken areas and escaped to London. It was clear that the joint commanders, William Pitt (Senior – the father of the Pennsylvania Pitt) and Robert Venables would need to add to their armies on the way, with men from Barbados or other colonies.

At that time, there was a system called indentured servitude that provided a low-cost workforce to wealthy English businessmen in British-owned territories. Criminals would be sentenced to five years of labour in the colonies, after which they would be freed and given a small piece of land. Other indentured servants were typically Irish, Scottish, or Welsh prisoners of war, who would similarly have signed a contract to work in servitude on the colonies. It was not exactly slavery - more like human trafficking, in which the worker goes to a more developed country from a poor one but must work for years to pay back the expenses incurred by the people running the operation. Pitt and Venables took advantage of this system to add to their ranks.

When Pitt and Venables arrived in Barbados they promised the indentured servants freedom from their contracts if they joined their army. It must have seemed like an upgrade in circumstance to the men, as around 4,000 men joined the British force. Obviously, this was a great loss to the Barbadian landowners, who were understandably furious, as they were being robbed of a great portion of their labourers.

In April 1655, the British fleet led by Pitt and Venables attacked Spanish-held Santo Domingo as per Cromwell's plan. The attack failed, partly because the weather had driven them further around the coast than they had wanted to land. Their attacking forces then had to march for three days through difficult terrain. The British lost 1,000 men, many from dehydration and dysentery - before they could fire a single shot. They made two attempts to capture Santo Domingo but were unsuccessful. The despondent Pitt and Venables could not return to Britain empty handed so they sailed on to attack the Spanish colony of Jamaica, which was far less fortified. The British quickly defeated the defending forces in Jamaica, capturing what is now called Spanish Town. However, their taste of success was short-lived. Slaves freed by the Spanish had fled into the hills and had joined forces with the Jamaican Maroons, and together they made it difficult for the English to control the interior. The occupying British troops did not have enough food to eat and had to send a party to Cayman to bring back turtle meat, as it was known to be in plentiful supply there. All the while, they were attacked by the Maroons. Within a year, the 7,000 men who had started the campaign dwindled down to 2,500 due to disease and malnutrition. It is not surprising that some left for the Cayman Islands and never returned.

It is thought that some of the early inhabitants of Cayman were deserters or ex-soldiers from Cromwell's army who had made their way two hundred miles further west, to a less troubled life. It is reported that in 1658 there were two prominent men living on the island. One was a Welshman called Walters (or Watler), and another man, named Bawden or Bodden. The common belief is that they had both been serving in Cromwell's army in Jamaica. The army was demobilised, and soldiers granted honourable discharges, from 1661 - so it is likely that soldiers who had left the army before that time may have been deserters – or perhaps the dates were wrong. Tradition also has it that Watler and Bawden were legitimate turtle fishermen, who travelled from island to island as was necessary, and eventually settled in Cayman because of its plentiful supply.

Late 17th Century to 1794

Towards the end of the 17th century, we know that the Spanish and the English had interests in Cayman. Islands, even today, are seen as being of strategic value against other nations, and the first Governor of Jamaica was told to treat Cayman as though they belonged to Britain. We also know that in 1667, five ships from Jamaica were seized by the Spanish in Cayman, and that in January 1668, the privateer Sir Henry Morgan used the islands as a base for his attack on Cuba.

The Treaty of Madrid was signed in July 1670 to stop further fighting between Britain and Spain. It stated that England should retain control of territories that it already owned in the Caribbean. From that day, the Cayman Islands were included along with Jamaica as British possessions – with Cayman being a dependency of Jamaica.

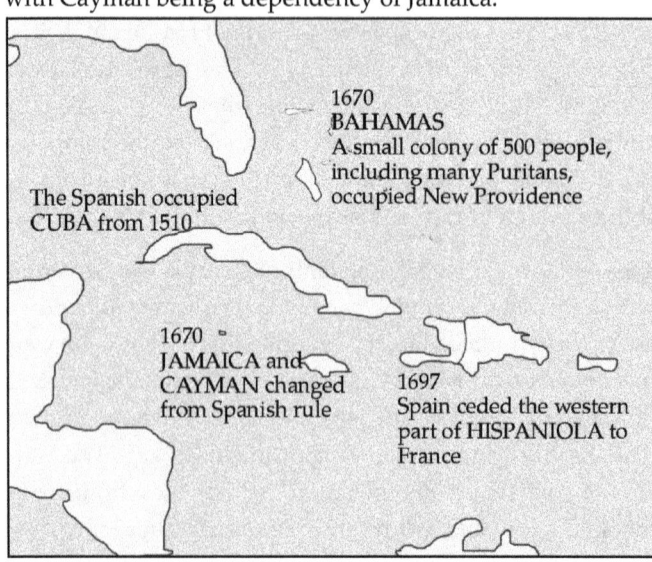

Map of the Greater Antilles referring to the colonial status of some Caribbean islands in the 16th and 17th Centuries

The first land grants in Cayman were recorded in the 1730s, when official settlement of Cayman began, but people had been living in Cayman well before that. This seems to have been the decade that saw the first slaves from Africa arrive in Cayman. Mostly men, they were forced to cut timber – probably mahogany for furniture, and fustic, also known as dyers' mulberry, for fabric dye.

In 1773, the first survey or "map" of Cayman was drawn by the Royal Navy. The population recorded at that time was 400, with half being free and half being slaves. Trading of cotton, turtle, sarsaparilla, and wood were being exported to Jamaica. In 1776 there was an addition to the Cayman population when Britain evacuated the Miskito Coast of Central America, having done a deal with Spain. Many moved along the coast to Belize, but some people settled in Jamaica and Cayman, and took with them their enslaved workers.

Wreck of The Ten Sail

8th February 1794

In November 1793, the British Royal Navy captured a French frigate, the 32-gun, 12-pounder, L'Inconstante, off the island of St. Domingue. The British re-named her HMS Convert. In February, the following year, she, and her experienced captain John Lawford, were ordered to escort a 6-vessel merchant convoy from Jamaica to Britain. A further three merchant ships needed to be escorted to the United States, so nine vessels, led by HMS Convert, headed on a course that would take them west, past the Cayman Islands.

After sailing for 24 hours and believing that he had already past the Cayman Islands, Lawford retired to his bed, after first giving orders to head a little more north, aiming, presumably for the Yucatan Channel, the strait between Mexico and Cuba. The change of direction sent the ships towards the reef at Gun Bay, East End. Shortly after 3:00 am a distress gun was fired as an alarm by one ship as it realised its predicament, but there was little to be done to avoid disaster. Some of the boats were already foundering on the rocks and strong currents were making the conditions treacherous. The Convert herself may have managed to avert running aground, but in the mayhem, darkness, and confusion it was rammed by a merchantman that had changed tack and was so forced onto the reef - where she was severely damaged.

The Caymanians of East End paddled out in canoes and open boats and rescued as many as four hundred and fifty sailors and passengers, including Lady Emilia Cooke. Remarkably, only eight souls were lost, including Captain Martin of HMS Britannia, who went down with his ship. Captain Lawford sent messages to Cuba and Jamaica for help, as the local people could only feed the survivors for a few days. Over the course of a few weeks, ships of various descriptions sailed to Cayman to pick up the survivors and to salvage what they could of the cargoes. In mid-March, HMS Success arrived to pick up the last remaining members of the shipwrecked crews, including Captain Lawford, who was taken back to Port Royal to be court martialled. He was acquitted of all charges.

Today, Cayman is a tax-free island, and it is a widely held belief that this stems from the heroism of the islanders during the wreck of the ten-sail disaster. The legend has it that there was a member of the royal family on board one of the vessels, whose life was saved in the rescue. King George III is said to have decreed that, as a reward, Caymanians should never be conscripted into war service nor be subject to paying taxes. There is no written documentary evidence to support this claim but, despite being a British Overseas Territory with all the benefits arising from such status, Cayman pays no taxes to Great Britain

The 19ᵗʰ Century

An 1802 census recorded the population of Grand Cayman as being 933, roughly half of whom were of British descent, the other half being slaves of African descent. Over half of these worked on cotton plantations. Five years later, in 1807, the Trans-Atlantic slave trade was abolished, which ended the transportation of slaves from Africa. However, slavery, and illegal human trafficking continued in the Americas. A later census in 1826 showed that over half of the population of Cayman were slaves. There were 889 slaves and 689 free persons (white and non-white) at that time.

Long Celia

It is hard to imagine being a slave, and how much one might long for liberty. How much harder it might have been to know that the world had begun to recognize that slavery was wrong and had abolished the slave trade and yet, more than a decade later, you still were not free. This was the position Celia Eden found herself in, in 1820. For years she had heard stories of rebellions and changes that were happening on other islands, and of the abolition movement, and had seen her hopes rise and be dashed time and time again.

One day, Celia had been talking with a black crewmember of a ship that had arrived from Jamaica. He told her that there was talk that the very next ship would be bringing the decree of emancipation. Indeed, some suspected that the decree had already arrived from England but had somehow been destroyed.

Celia excitedly shared this news with a neighbour, Sarah Harbourn, who promptly reported her to the authorities. Harbourn's testimony referred to some remarks that Long Celia had made about it being pointless for the white masters to keep hiding the truth about the emancipation and claimed Celia had said that once the decree arrived "Let two negroes go to the house with machetes, they would run." This was sufficient for Long Celia to be

142

arrested for trying to 'stir up a revolution'. She was found guilty by fourteen white, slave-holding men and harshly punished, even by the standards of the time. She was stripped naked in a public place in George Town and whipped fifty times. Poor Celia had to spend fifteen more years as a slave before being emancipated, and only lived a further five years as a free woman.

In 2003, Long Celia was included in the Cayman Islands Wall of Honour, in George Town.

Wrecking, Turtling, and Cotton

It is quite ironic that Cayman remembers so well the heroism of the night that it saved the passengers and crew of the British ship HMS Convert, when one of its economic mainstays at the time was the business of wrecking. Locals would deliberately lure ships onto the reefs and would gain from the salvaged contents of the wrecked ships and from the skills of any of those rescued if they chose to stay on the islands. One such event was reported by a Presbyterian missionary, Hope Waddell, who was rescued from a schooner that ran aground off East End in 1845.

A fleet of canoes was making for us, and soon surrounded our helpless craft; when a host of wild, ruthless-looking coloured men sprang up the sides, like pirates or boarders greedy for prey. The head man, advancing to the captain, with one word of pity and two of business, agreed to take everything ashore, on the usual terms of half for their trouble. (Hannerz, 1974)

Wrecks, and subsequent 'rescues' by Caymanian vessels near Cuba, were sufficiently frequent that a Spanish, Cuban official saw the Caymanian people as lawless thieves posing as fishermen, writing to Spain that they should be wiped out. This may explain why there were attacks on Cayman in the late eighteenth and early nineteenth centuries.

In those early days of settlement in Cayman, other sources of revenue were turtling – which involved selling turtle meat to passing ships, and farming. There was some small-scale cattle and pig farming, which is why the Hogsties or Hog Stye Bay in George Town was so named, but the land, generally, was not ideal for crops. In the early nineteenth century there was a great demand for cotton in Europe and the land in Cayman was of sufficient quality that it could be used to grow cotton. Along with cotton production came the need for labour, so Cayman's slave population reached its peak at this time.

Ultimately, Cayman could not compete with much larger organisations such as the plantations in the southern states of America. Cayman reverted to subsistence farming, and it is said that the landowners in Cayman were so poor that their slaves had to provide their own soap to do their masters' laundry.

Questions

1. What might have been used to make soap in the 1800s?

a) Animal fats   b) Oil from vegetables and nuts   c) Lye or potash

2. According to the WWF, what is the status of the green turtle?

 a) critically endangered   b) endangered   c) vulnerable

3. Which of these places was also known for wrecking ships to bolster their local economy?

a) Cornwall, UK b) San Francisco, USA   c) Rome, Italy

d) The Bahamas   e) Germany   f) Florida Keys   g) Devon, UK

answers on page 164

The Abolition of Slavery – 1834

From midnight on July 31st, 1834, slavery became illegal across the British Empire. However, this did not mean that slaves became free men and women. They were to continue to work for their former masters as apprentices for a further six years. Slave-owners across the empire would be compensated by the British government for the loss of their registered slaves. However, Cayman had not registered their slaves, so those in Cayman were not bound to the apprenticeship system and became emancipated after just ten months – much to the dismay of their former masters.

At this point, there was a lot of movement of people around the Cayman Islands. Some former slaves claimed less inhabited land to the north and east of Grand Cayman. Some, perhaps the Scott, Ritch, and Foster families, travelled to Cayman Brac in search of better agricultural land. It is thought that some escaped slaves from Cuba may have made the passage to the sister islands too. Turtling, again, became a major commercial interest for Grand Cayman, while the sister islands focused on growing coconuts.

Late 19th Century

Nothing much happened in Cayman for decades in the mid-1800s. It craved connection with the world but saw fewer passing ships during the age of steam than it did in the age of sail, as it was then possible to bypass Cayman altogether without need to stock up on provisions. Cayman repeatedly reached out to Jamaica with their concerns.

The *Act for the Government of the Cayman Islands* became law on 22nd June 1863, stating that all British laws that were valid in Jamaica also applied to the Cayman Islands. The Governor of Jamaica would exercise authority in the Cayman Islands as if they were part of Jamaica, and the Supreme Court of Jamaica would also have jurisdiction over the Caymanian legal system.

Tradition, by Simon Morris - 2003

During the Ten-Years War of 1868-1878, when Cuba was battling for independence from Spain, a ban was put on any non-Spanish ships from entering the waters near Cuba. This hampered turtling and wrecking for a while, though it did continue to a lesser extent, even after the Cubans seized a Caymanian vessel, The Star. Turtling near Cuba came finally to an end after the Spanish-American War in 1898, with a stricter ban on foreign ships imposed by Cuba.

19th Century Hurricanes

Towards the end of the Ten Years War, in 1876 and 1877, there were severe hurricanes in the region. This image shows one hurricane starting north of Panama, travelling north, and going straight over Cayman a major hurricane. It destroyed 170 homes on Grand Cayman.

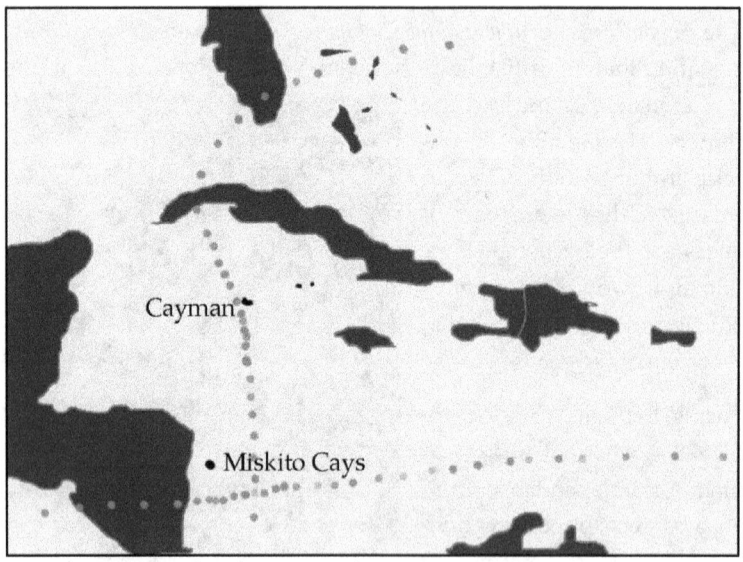

The tracks of two major hurricanes in 1876 and 1877

A major hurricane the following year, 1877, sank nine of twenty Caymanian boats catching turtles at the Miskito Cays, off Nicaragua, with the loss of 64 lives.

Stamps

It may be difficult to imagine, looking at Cayman as it is today, that at one time it had almost no economy at all – and was living a hand-to-mouth existence. Meagre forms of income emerged around the turn of the century - some were short-lived, while others lasted longer. For a few years, Cayman was able to export phosphate fertiliser made from calcium carbonate and guano, until it became easier and cheaper for customers to buy it from Florida. Honey production began at this time and became a small but steady source of revenue. Cayman still produces great honey. By far the greatest source of income though, which lasted for decades, was when Cayman set up post offices and started printing postage stamps.

Cayman stamps became much sought-after items by collectors. They came from a new source, with a British connection, and bore the head of the monarch – beginning with Queen Victoria. In the financial year 1913-1914, over 35% of the Cayman government's revenue came from the sale of stamps.

Aside from the attraction of stamps combining scenes of a tropical island with the heads of British royalty, there was another reason for collectors to want postcards and letters from Cayman. You may know that there is a limestone (ironshore) rock-formation in West Bay that is said to resemble the fires of Hell – well, there is a post office right beside it. Mail sent from there not only bears a Cayman postage stamp but has the postmark which shows that the correspondence came from Hell itself – making it very collectable.

Stamp Question:

The *Treskilling Yellow* and *The Inverted Jenny* are stamps that would easily fetch over a million dollars at auction. Part of their high value comes from an attribute that they share. What do they have in common?

answer on page 164

Connected to the World – and then The Depression

After the Great War, over 3,000 Caymanian men emigrated to earn money overseas – with most going to the USA. The remittances they sent back became a major part of Cayman's economy. In 1927, Cayman's connection with the world was made easier by the introduction of a regular steamboat operating between Cayman and Jamaica. Shortly afterwards, a route between Tampa and George Town was established. All was going well, until the Great Depression struck. Men returned from America, but still had difficulty making a living in Cayman as there was hardly any work, and even the demand for turtle meat was very limited.

American Farmer during the Great Depression - Photo: Library of Congress

The 1932 Hurricane

The hurricane of 1932 gets a mention elsewhere in this book, but it is included here as it helps to indicate that, when we think that things can not get much worse, they can! Not only were the people of Cayman battered by an economic crisis in the early 1930s, but they were at the mercy of the powerful, tropical weather.

The 1932 Cuba Hurricane, as it is recorded, battered the three Cayman Islands for over two days – destroying homes, ships, and livelihoods. Fortunately, only one life was lost on Grand Cayman, but the storm moved on and hit the sister islands with greater force.

The cemetery on low-lying Little Cayman was washed away, leaving corpses in the street. The well water across the island was contaminated, and much of the landscape flattened. The bluff on the Brac had provided some shelter from the tidal surge and the high winds, but after the eye of the storm passed some Brackers left the safety of the bluff and were caught by the second attack of the hurricane, with 69 being killed on the island.

The final death toll, and loss to the community, was more than is indicated by the number of those who died on Cayman Brac. Many of Cayman Brac's menfolk were away from home, fishing, - and forty more were lost at sea. Seven more Brackers were working in Santa Cruz and were killed by the storm - along with 2,500 Cubans.

1. **How high is the highest point above sea level on Little Cayman?**
   a) 40 feet (12m)   b) 80 feet (24m)   c) 120 feet (36m)

2. **Choose the closest estimate of the distance in nautical miles from Cayman Brac to Santa Cruz, Cuba.**
   a) 80 miles   b) 120 miles   c) 180 miles   d) 270 miles

answers on page 164

1934 - Commissioner Cardinall

Great Britain helped Cayman get back on her feet after the 1932 Hurricane, although, because of poor communications at the time, it took a while for the plight of Cayman and the sister islands to become known. Ships were sent from Jamaica carrying food supplies and tents, and a medical officer for the injured. They were joined by a Royal Navy ship, the HMS Dragon, which had a desalination plant aboard and could provide the islands with drinking water. The Navy left after they had helped to fix wells and cisterns.

The appointment of a Commissioner to Cayman just two years after the hurricane, in 1934, was a major step forward for the islands. He oversaw the construction and development of much-needed infrastructure. This included government buildings, a hospital, town halls which could double as schools and hurricane shelters, and a better road system. Commissioner Cardinall also set up a radio communications system, with a link to Cayman Brac. He even used the popular entertainment device, the wireless radio, to push Cayman as a tourist destination, informing listeners that it had probably the best bathing beach in the world. Cardinall was instrumental in arranging for the first visit by a cruise ship to Cayman – SS Atlantis, in 1937.

The almost completed, pedestrianised Cardinall Avenue, September 2022

Tourism

Planes, Condominiums and Mosquitoes

1950s – 1990s

By 1950, a retired Royal Air Force Wing Commander, Owen Roberts, had established a weekly seaplane service connecting Grand Cayman with Tampa, Florida, and Kingston, Jamaica. He lobbied for an airstrip to be built on Grand Cayman and the first plane touched down at the new airport in 1953. Roberts, himself, had piloted the scheduled, inaugural flight from Kingston in April 1953, but it never made it to Cayman – it crashed shortly after take-off, killing Roberts and twelve others.

In the mid-50s, LACSA, the Costa Rican airline, was operating regular flights from San Jose, Costa Rica, stopping off at Grand Cayman and Havana, Cuba on the way to Miami. BWIA introduced a non-stop flight between Cayman and Miami in 1958. This was also the year that Miss Hebe Connors opened her 8-room guest house on South Church Street – Sunset House.

At that time, in Cayman, war was being waged against mosquitoes. The Mosquito Control Research Unit (MRCU) was set up in 1965 and 'fogging' (spraying insecticides from trucks) began in 1966. Spraying from Cessna aircraft began in 1971. The mosquito problem was one that needed to be solved if Cayman were to become a first-class tourist destination. The MRCU still operates today, to protect the islands from, not only the unpleasantness of bites as we sip our evening cocktails, but from threats such as zika and malaria.

The mid-60s was also around the same time that passengers began arriving on jet aircraft, rather than propeller planes. Cayman Airways was founded in 1968, when the CI Government bought 51% of Cayman Brac Airways from LACSA. Southern Airways was the first US-based airline to add a Cayman route in the 1970s, continuing as Northwest Airlines in the

1980s. Cayman Airways became wholly government owned in 1977. Its first passenger jet acquisition was in 1978, with a service to Houston, Texas. American Airlines, Pan Am, and Eastern Airlines all had scheduled flights by 1989.

Through this period, hotels and condominiums began appearing on 7-Mile Beach, and the battle against mosquitoes was being won by the MRCU. The table below shows a selection of the hotels, condominiums and time-shares that sprung up in the 1970s and early '80s.

By 1980 there were over 120,000 visitors arriving by air and almost 61,000 visitors arriving by cruise ship. In 2005 there were about 300,000 arrivals by air, and 1.8 million by cruise ship. In 2019 (the year before Covid) there were 500,000 air arrivals and 1.8 million by cruise ship.

Selected Condominiums and Hotels between 1950-1982

Complex / resort	Date built
Poinsettia	1982
Cayman Reef Resort	1982
Plantana	1982
Tamarind Bay	1982
The Anchorage	1980
White Sands	1980
Villas of the Galleon	1980
Lacovia	1979
Island Pines	1979
Seagull Condominiums	1978
The Christopher Columbus	1978
Silver Sands	1978
Holiday Inn Hotel	1973
Harbour Heights	1971
Laguna del Mar	1969
Galleon Beach Hotel	1950

As a further indicator of how tourism is still on the increase in Cayman, new, bigger hotels are constantly being added. The Ritz-Carlton opened on 7-Mile Beach in 2006, on the site of the original Holiday Inn. It has 363 rooms and 69 luxury residences. The 264-room, Kimpton Seafire Resort and Spa opened in 2016, with the Residences at Seafire opening the following year. A new Grand Hyatt hotel and residences is due to be finished before 2024, and three other ten-storey hotels are currently under construction.

Construction underway along West Bay Road in September, 2022

Finance

Cayman's Rise as an Offshore Financial Services Centre

1950s – today

Caymanian men worked in the American merchant navy, before, during and after World War II. Two-thirds of Cayman's men fought for Britain during the war, which is an extraordinarily high proportion. After the war, Caymanians found jobs on shipping lines and working for oil companies. They were highly valued, and they sent a lot of money home. This was a boom time for Cayman, and in 1953, Barclays opened the first public bank on Grand Cayman. Two more retail banks opened ten years later.

Things were changing politically during the late 1950s. There was an attempt to make a unified Caribbean state out of the colonised countries in the Caribbean, and 1958 saw the inauguration of a group of 10 countries, allied as the West Indies Federation. Jamaica was one of these countries, and Cayman was a dependency of Jamaica. A delegation was sent from Cayman to negotiate for its autonomy - it wanted to continue to run certain things itself and break away from Jamaica. This came to pass in 1959 when Cayman received its own constitution from a Royal Order-in-Council. Jamaica still retained some authority over Cayman, but when Jamaica became independent in 1962 a decision was made by Cayman to break away, while retaining their links with Great Britain. This was a major step forward. In 1966, the Banks and Trust Companies Law was enacted, making foreign investment possible.

Since 1971, Cayman has had a Governor, acting as the British monarch's representative in charge of the civil service, the police force, external affairs, and internal security Also in 1971, Cayman introduced the Cayman Islands dollar – and fixed this new currency to the US dollar. In 1979 the financial sector diversified with the Insurance Law. By 1989, Cayman was the world's second largest insurance centre.

The stability of the connection with Britain, as a dependent territory, provided confidence to the financial industry. Also, Cayman benefits from having less class inequality, based on skin colour, than other Caribbean Islands. No wealthy aristocratic capitalists had set up huge cotton or sugar plantations, and the 'wealthy' white landowners in Cayman were not much better off than anyone else after emancipation. According to the CIA factbook, the racial demographic of Cayman is 40% mixed, 20% white, 20% black and 20% 'various.' Early investors would not have seen any threat to stability on racial, or class divide, terms.

The people with power in Cayman had not been handed their status by Great Britain, they had earned it through being entrepreneurs and merchants. In the 1950s, these leaders of industry and commerce assumed positions as Justices of the Peace, even though they had no legal training, which then led to roles in the governing body of Cayman, the Legislative Assembly. This autonomy, away from the bureaucracy of Britain, allowed them flexibility to change with the times – and because they were so heavily involved in their capitalist ventures with strong links to the financial sector, they were quick to respond favourably whenever needed.

The historical connection that Cayman had with the USA was another factor in Cayman's success. Most of Cayman's revenue would eventually come from its partnership with America, and Cayman was aware of this from the early days. American banker John Mathewson asserted in 1999 that 98% of deposits in Cayman's banks came from American investors. Also, the proximity of Cayman to the USA, including the time-zone, should not be overlooked.

Even if Cayman had not noticed the importance of the United States to its economy, it was aware that it had almost no economy of its own and needed to be connected to other nations – as it had been in the past. It is impressive that Cayman transitioned from having a reputation gained by a form of piracy, earned by the deliberate wrecking and 'rescuing' of passing ships, through the early days of being a tax haven frequently associated with money laundering for organised crime syndicates, to the highly respected offshore centre that it is today – all within three generations.

Evolving with America as an ally, while aiding companies and individuals that hide money from Uncle Sam, has taken a great deal of skill. In the 1970s, offshore centres like those in the Bahamas and Cayman were seen by some US offices as being accessories to financial crime. In 1976, protecting their clients from the US authorities, Cayman's banking secrecy laws which were already tight, were tightened. America needed evidence of criminal activity by the Mafia, drug barons and corrupt leaders of nations, so its response was to impose massive fines on any part of the banking operations that were on US soil, flexing its considerable muscle. Some sort of compromise had to be struck, and a way forward was agreed in 1986. Cayman became more diligent in anti-money laundering practices – more so than other offshore centres, and America was happy for a while.

While some tax havens had been receiving citations and penalties for non-compliance with the US General Accounting Office, Cayman had been leading the way with increased regulation against shell corporations. It was also doing it by directly dealing with the United States, rather than involving Britain's Foreign and Commonwealth Office. Cayman was staying ahead of the game on a more global basis too, with promises to the Paris-based Organisation for Economic Development and Cooperation (OECD) to further commit to addressing criminal tax matters by 2003.

Improving compliance made perfect sense. The Financial Times in 1997 had reported that Cayman's offshore centre was dominated by mutual funds and Eurobonds, rather than personal, oligarch-type, banking. Cayman's government minister pointed out that 85% of Cayman banking came from firms conducting 'institutional business' – so complying with the OECD would not have a significant effect. Distancing itself away from anything illicit would attract more investors at an institutional level. However, around the turn of the millennium, Cayman had not done quite enough to satisfy the US Department of Treasury's Financial Crimes Enforcement Network,

(FINCEN) and found itself on a blacklist issued by the international Financial Action Task Force (FATF). As a measure of Cayman's astuteness and adaptability, Cayman fixed what it needed to fix and was removed from the list in June 2001.

At times, in Cayman, there has been some local sentiment in favour of seeking independence from Great Britain – mainly by residents outside the finance industry. These ideas have been summarily quashed - nipped in the bud by ministers who have understood that even the merest glimpse of Cayman pulling away from the stability provided by Britain would send investors scurrying away almost immediately. When the Bahamas declared independence in 1973 it dropped from the fourth largest offshore centre to the eleventh. Cayman's laws, including laws regarding secrecy in Cayman banks, derive from English common law – which is the style of law practised in most of Britain's former colonies, including America. Cayman is not untouchable by US-based authorities but being aligned with Britain offers the small dependent territory a great deal of protection.

Since the dawn of the tax haven, the authorities who would seek to gather more tax have continually been changing the regulations to gain access to the information they require, and the haven has tried to protect its clients' interests. Whereas Cayman may have had some involvement with pirates in the past, the Cayman of today – and every other tax haven, is more about helping giant corporations bury their treasure - while avoiding heavy punishments for non-compliance. Cayman has become an industry leader in this cat-and-mouse game.

Cayman's success in the finance field has come from its ability to adapt and diversify, while strengthening what it does best - staying one step ahead of its competitors. The Cayman Islands Stock Exchange (CSX) was founded in 1996 and was granted organisation status by the London Stock Exchange in 1999. By 2022 the CSX has listed more than 7,300 securities and maintained a market capitalisation of more than US$804 billion. By 2017, around 85% of the world's hedge funds were domiciled in the Cayman Islands. Over the last twenty years, Cayman has been building up its portfolio so that it now offers services in banking, trust companies, mutual funds, company management, structured financing, shipping registration, accounting, insurance, and securities listings on the stock exchange – with all the experts, accountants, managers, lawyers, and personnel the industry could ever need, living in high style in the tiny Caribbean paradise.

Test your knowledge of accountancy history. Try to complete the blanks about the mergers of some of the big firms.

a) 1998 Price Waterhouse merged with Coopers and _____ to form PWC.

b) 1993 The international firm of Deloitte Touche _____ was named.

c) 1989 Deloitte and _____ merged with Touche _____ to form Deloitte and Touche

d) 1989 Ernst and_____ and Arthur Young and Co. merged to form Ernst and Young.

answers on page 164

Local Heroes

Throughout Cayman's history some big decisions were made that steered the country along its relatively successful course. Policymakers were responsible for keeping ties with Britain, starting up the island as a tourist destination, ridding the country of mosquitoes, building the airport, and establishing the country as a financial centre – but who played which role?

Here are snippets taken from biographies of three of Cayman's national heroes, taken from CI Government websites.

Match these three biographies to the names of the corresponding national heroes.

Choose from:

A. Mr. Ormond L. Panton, OBE

B. The Hon. James (Jim) Manoah Bodden

C. William Warren Conolly, OBE

D. Mr. Thomas William Farrington, CBE, JP

1. This person was Cayman's first National Hero, honoured with a state funeral and, later, a statue in Heroes Square in the centre of George Town. In his time as the minister responsible for tourism and aviation, this visionary was instrumental in establishing Cayman Airways and constructing Owens Roberts International Airport.

This statue in George Town depicts one of Cayman's national heroes – but which one?

2. This attorney founded Cayman's first political party and was the first politician to win an election as party leader. He introduced a motion to allow Cayman authorities to issue US visa waivers, thereby facilitating merchant marine employment for Caymanians.

3. This national hero set in motion some of the country's key legislation, including the bank & trust companies, land adjudication and registered land laws. He was instrumental in creating the Department of Tourism and the crucial Mosquito Control and Natural Resources Department. He also spearheaded the official introduction of Cayman Islands currency in May 1972 and oversaw the completion of the Legislative Assembly building, the Port Authority finger pier and warehouse, the old Government Administration Building and the Courts Building.

answers on page 164

Who was Premier?

Who was the premier when these major events took place?

a) Hurricane Ivan

b) The Covid-19 lockdown

c) The death of Her Majesty, Queen Elizabeth II

answers on page 164

Answers for Chapter 9

Page 131. Las Tortugas

Page 132. Cayman Brac and Little Cayman

Page 133. The English explorer was Francis Drake

Page 134. Harvey (medicine), Caravaggio (art), Galileo (astronomy)

       Bacon (science), Shakespeare (literature)

Page 145. a) All 3 of these   b) endangered

       c) Cornwall, Bahamas, Florida Keys, Devon

Page 149. They both are rare because they were printed imperfectly and were distributed before anyone realised. The Inverted Jenny has a depiction of a biplane printed upside-down, and the Treskilling Yellow should be green.

Page 151. 1. 40 feet (12m)   2. 120 nautical miles

P160   a) Lybrand b) Tohmatsu c) Haskins   Ross   d) Whinney

Page 161-162   1. Jim Bodden (statue)

          2. Ormond L. Panton

          3. William Warren Conolly

Page 162. a) McKeeva Bush   b) Alden McLaughlin   c) Wayne Panton

CHAPTER TEN

Living in Cayman

The Climate

Cayman is in the tropics, which means that it lies between the Tropic of Capricorn, south of the equator, and the Tropic of Cancer, north of the equator. The tropics include all the areas on the Earth where the Sun contacts a point directly overhead at least once during the solar year - which means that the latitude of the tropics is roughly equal to the angle of the tilt of the Earth's axis. The Tropic of Cancer is about 23.5° north of the equator – Cayman is close to 19° north. It is somewhere between warm and hot all year around in Cayman.

Hot weather

Match the record <u>high</u> temperatures with the correct country

113°F   in 1937   _____

101.7°F in 2019   _____

94.8°F   in 2016   _____

Canada   England   Grand Cayman

answers on page 182

Cool Weather

Because of its location, the length of days (from sunrise to sunset) does not vary much throughout the year in Cayman. The longest day is 13 hours and 20 minutes, while the shortest day is 11 hours – basically one hour either side of a 12-hour day. Also, Cayman's daily temperatures are very consistent at around mid-80s to mid-90s, so expect to see locals feeling the cold and wearing jackets when the mercury dips below 80 degrees.

Cooler weather in Cayman tends to be from November through until Easter. Winter brings the Christmas breeze – cooler air and lower humidity that everyone loves. Nor'westers, when they occur, tend to bring some cooler but more dramatic weather, and a change of wind direction - from the Northwest.

Having said all this there are exceptions to every rule. Check out the low temperatures in the list below and try the challenge.

Match the record low temperatures with the correct country

52°F	in 1968	_____
43.3° F	in 1961	_____
34.7°F	in 2017	_____
12°F	in 1979	_____

Choose from: **Cayman**   **Philippines**   **Qatar**   **Hawaii**

answers on page 182

Death Statistics

Cayman is, generally, a safe place to live. Here are a few statistics that confirm this, and a couple that might be surprising. The data for the UK, USA, Jamaica, and China are included for comparison.

	Cayman	USA	UK	China	Jamaica
Infant mortality rate per 100,000	5.6	5.6	3.7	12	12
Life expectancy at birth	81	80	81	76	74
Homicides per 100,000	8.4 *	5	1.2	0.5	47
Gun related death rate per 100,000	5 *	12.2	0.2	0.16	Not available but very high
Road accident fatality rate per 100,000 people / (10,000 vehicles in brackets)	15 (per vehicle data not available)	12.4 (14)	2.9 (5.7)	17.8 (104)	11.5 (62)
Crude death rate (2019) (per 1,000 pop.)	3.3	8.8	9.4	7.1	7.6
COVID-19 Deaths per million** Sept 11th, 2022	431	3213	2760	4	1100

*The apparent, relatively high homicide and shooting rates shown here for Cayman are due to a handful of deaths per year caused by grievances between rival members of small criminal groups. In some years there are no gun deaths at all, but in 2010 there were seven. There are small 'gangs' in Cayman, but they do not have a great impact on the general population. As in most places, their violence tends to be levelled at each other more than the public.

Mortality data for the Cayman Islands show that in 2005 the leading causes of death were cancers, ischemic heart disease, cerebrovascular diseases, and diabetes.

Traffic fatalities are consistently the main cause of accidental death, but there are also 4-6 deaths by drowning each year in Cayman. Typically, these are older tourists who get into difficulty snorkelling or scuba diving.

Killers in Cayman

Of the animal families that kill the most humans, four of them can be found in Cayman. Snakes kill about 100,000 people worldwide every year. Luckily, the species of snakes that live in Cayman are not venomous or harmful to humans, so we do not have to worry about them. What about the other three animal families on the list?

There is no need to worry. The threat to human life that two of them pose is kept in check by science and control strategies. Unfortunately, the other animal (B), accounts for about 6 deliberate deaths per year in Cayman - but these creatures are more lethal in many other countries.

The missing animal names from the list below are all in the top five most prolific killers of humans on the planet – some from the diseases they carry, rather than from the animal itself.

Name the animals, A, B and C. Also, name the cause of death, D.

Rank	Animal	Deaths per year worldwide	Cause of Death
1	A	725,000- 1 million	Malaria, dengue fever
2	B	475,000	D
3	**Snakes**	100,000	Anaphylactic reaction. Kidney or heart muscle failure.
4	C	35,000	Rabies
5	Freshwater snails	2,000-200,000	Parasitic disease
6	Assassin (Kissing) Bug	12,000	Chagas Disease
7	Tsetse Fly	10,000	Sleeping sickness - coma

answer on page 182

Dangerous Plants

There are some lethal plants on the island, and a few others that can have very unpleasant effects on an unsuspecting human. Here are a few of the worst.

Manchineel

Severe blistering/ burning of the skin
Eating the fruit will cause blisters inside the mouth
Eating the fruit can cause death
Smoke from burning the wood can cause blindness – inhaling the smoke can cause blistering.
Never shelter from the rain under a manchineel. Sap that drips on you will blister your skin.

John Crow Bead or 'Crab's Eyes' or Indian Licorice or Rosary Pea

The seeds of the *Abrus precatorius* are red with a black spot and are deadly poisonous. They contain the toxin abrin, which is similar to ricin. If it gets straight into your bloodstream through an open cut it could be fatal. If eaten, the poison can cause renal failure leading to death, and there is no antidote. Do not be tempted to eat wild berries in Cayman!

Castor Oil Plant, Castor Bean

The bean-like seeds from this plant contain the toxin ricin. Castor oil when properly processed has healing properties, but these seeds can be fatal if swallowed. The best way for the ricin to enter the system is through inhalation or injection, which should be very unlikely. There is no antidote, but there are ways of treating the symptoms, but if they do not work, death would probably come through respiratory failure. Thankfully, most residents and visitors tend to avoid such a fate.

Poison Tree

This one might not kill you, but it has a poisonous sap that will cause itches, burns and blistering, similar to poison ivy.

Maiden Plum

Maiden plum has easily damaged leaves which leak their sap onto skin. Most people have an allergic reaction to this sap. The trouble with this one is that it does not hurt on contact – so you may be walking through an area with maiden plum with no awareness of your plight until it hits you later. Sores appear after about 24 hours and become more inflamed over the next week or two.

Coconuts

Although it has been said that falling coconuts kill ten times more people each year than sharks, there is little evidence to support this claim. Shark deaths are well documented and only average about four per year. There are about 60 shark attacks per year, with about 50 of those being in waters off the USA and Australia, and only a couple being off Caribbean islands. Statistics are not really collated on 'death by coconut', but each country and island on which they grow will have a story of a person being injured or killed by such a falling fruit. Fortunately, most of those anecdotes will be about an isolated incident many years ago – they are not common occurrences. Even so, it is probably not the best idea to walk or lie directly under a tree laden with coconuts.

If you have ever heard the thud of a heavy coconut as it hits the ground, you will appreciate how much it would hurt. From 5-metres high, a falling 2 kg coconut could hit the unsuspecting head of a sunbather with an energy of around 98 joules. Would that be sufficient to kill a person? One website, dedicated to researching impacts of remote-controlled planes hitting people in parks, shared that it was commonly accepted that an object striking a person's head with an energy greater than 80 joules had a 20% chance of being fatal. This rose to a 90% chance of death if the energy was more than 150 joules! If the 2 kg coconut fell from a greater height, say 10m, its energy would be more like 200 joules!

Places in Cayman

Where is that? Anagrams

How well do you know Cayman? Here are some anagrams to solve of well-known place names in Grand Cayman.

1. MOP IT RUN   _____ _____

2. SET COPS BATH   _____ _____

3. PREP COST   _____

4. SAD TEEN   _____ _____

5. BAA CYAN MA   _____ _____

6. ONE USES HUTS   _____ _____

7. ENVIABLE SCHEME   _____ _____ _____

8. ITCH MOVES   _____ _____

9. NO EGG TOWER   _____ _____

10. THIRD NOSE   _____ _____

answer on page 182

Where was that? Old Photos

Try to identify these Cayman locations from photographs taken in the 1980s and 1990s.

1. _____

2. _____

3. _____

4. _____

5. _____

6. _____

7. _____

answer on page 182

Places and Institutions

Cayman has a turtle centre and an iguana sanctuary. It also has a botanic park, but does it have a zoo? You might be surprised what it has and does not have.

Identify the **ten** places or facilities that CAN be found in Cayman.

Bowling Alley	**Ski Slope**
Hot Air Balloon Ride	**Railway Station**
Art Gallery	**Hyperbaric Chamber**
Baseball Diamond	**American Football Field**
Squash Club	**Racquetball Club**
Uber Ride Service	**Airbnb**
Cricket Pitch	**Athletics Stadium**
McDonald's Restaurant	**IHOP**
Cathedral	**Casino**
Cable car ride	**Museum**
Theatre	**15-storey building**

Public or Sports Club 50-Metre Swimming Pool

answer on page 182

Religion, Politics and Law in Cayman

By far the predominant faith in Cayman is Christianity, with about two-thirds of adherents being Protestant. This includes 23% belonging to the Church of God, and about 10% being Seventh Day Adventists. Roman Catholics account for 14%, and with recent influxes of workers from India and the Philippines the religions of these minority groups can now be added to the diversity. The official percentage of 'no religion' or atheist is about 10%, but if non-practising Christians were included in this category this would undoubtedly rise significantly.

Conservative followers of Christianity in Cayman, and more generally throughout the rest of the Caribbean, are finding it difficult to reconcile their interpretation of teachings of the Bible and some human rights issues, such as gay marriage. This has caused considerable tension and division in Cayman, which is a British Dependent Territory and follows English common law. In 2020, the Legislative Assembly of the Cayman Islands voted narrowly against a Domestic Partnership Bill which would have allowed gay couples similar rights to married couples. Politicians blocking the bill stated that they were doing so on religious grounds. However, as Cayman is a British Dependent Territory and Britain operates under the terms of the European Convention on Human Rights, the governor of the islands His Excellency Martin Roper had to intercede. As the UK's representative he exercised his constitutional prerogative to overrule the decision made by the local Legislative Assembly and enact, using his Reserve Powers, what is now known as the Civil Partnership Law, giving same-sex couples a status "functionally equivalent to marriage."

When the Legislative Assembly voted against the Civil Partnership Law, Cayman's Premier, Alden McLaughlin said that he was "utterly humiliated" by cabinet members who believed "that the government was free to decide which categories of people are entitled to enjoy the constitutionally guaranteed right to private and family life", pointing out that "Cayman is a democracy, not a theocracy."

How Many Churches?

The architectural terms, mosque, temple, and synagogue may be deceptively grand if used to describe the relatively humble buildings in which believers of these faiths worship in Cayman, but there are buildings in the communities dedicated as religious centres for Judaism and Islam.

Christian churches are much more in evidence, and it is difficult to drive even for five minutes and not pass a church of one kind or another. Some of these too, are humble. and not much more than someone's home with a sign over the door, but most are the size one might expect to see in a village or small town. These have thriving congregations and are highly social places full of singing and happy worshippers.

One of Grand Cayman's many churches

Grand Cayman is an island with an area of 76 square miles. Guess how many churches it has.

    a) 32   b) 76   c) 150   d) 200

answer on page 182

Nationalities

Caymanians make up 62.4% of the population of Cayman.

Choose from the nationalities in the list to complete the table.

Nationality	% of the population
Caymanians	62.4%
	16.4%
	5.7%
	2.4%
	1.7%
Other expat group	11.4%

American, British, Canadian, Filipino, Indian, Jamaican, South African

Surnames

When it comes to surnames, everyone knows that Ebanks and Bodden are the 2 most common surnames of people living in Cayman.

Which of the following surnames was <u>third</u> most common in 2020?

a) Kirkconnell   b) Smith   c) Watler

Which four of the following surnames also made the top ten list?

Brown   Scott   Hydes   McLaughlin

Bush   Thompson   Rankine   Foster

answer on page 182

Population of Cayman

The population of Cayman has been rising steadily since the 1950s.

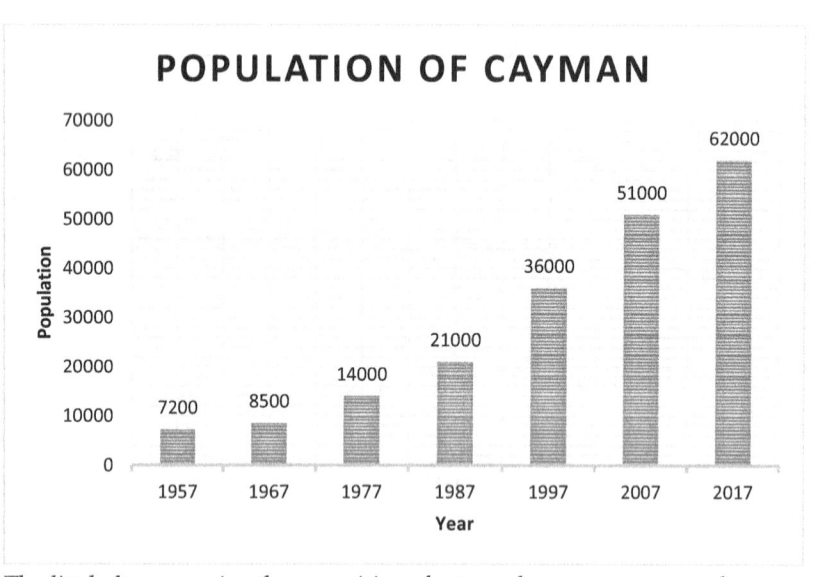

The list below contains the capacities of arts and sports venues and institutions around the world on par with the population of Cayman in each of the seven years shown in the graph. See if you can match them up.

Centre Court, Wimbledon, London (Tennis)

Adelaide Oval, Australia (Cricket)

Cambridge University staff and enrolled students, England

Inmate population at the Curran-Fromhold Correctional Facility, Pennsylvania, USA

Tottenham Hotspur Stadium, London (Football)

Symphony of the Seas (Cruise Ship)

United Center - Chicago Bulls (Basketball)

answers on page 182

Other Vital Statistics

Here are a few more snippets of information about Cayman that might be of interest.

	Cayman	USA	UK	China	Jamaica
GDP per capita (adjusted for purchasing power parity – World Bank 2019)	$72,481	$65,281	$48,710	$16,785	$10,166
Doctors per 10,000 people (WHO 2019) *(PAHO 2015)	55*	26	28	20	13
New AIDS/HIV cases per year per 100,000	5	518	665	10	40
Pupil-teacher ratio (primary) 2018 (World Bank)	16	14	20	16	25

WHO is the World Health Organization

PAHO is the Pan American Health Organization

Answers for Chapter 10

Page 165. 94.8°F was the record for Grand Cayman
101.7°F England   113°F Canada   (as of 2022)

Page 166. Reading the countries from left to right matches the temperatures from top to bottom: Cayman (52° F.) Philippines (43.3° F.) Qatar (34.7° F.) Hawaii (12° F.)

Page 169. A. Mosquitoes. Malaria was eradicated from Cayman in the early 1950s. However, if travellers from other islands have the disease it can be spread by a mosquito sucking their blood and infecting another person. There are about 3 imported cases per year. Worldwide, mosquito-transmitted malaria is a mass killer.

B. Humans   C. Dogs (carrying rabies) 95% of all rabies deaths are in Africa and Asia   D. Homicide/murder

Page 173.   1. Rum Point 2. Spotts Beach 3.Prospect 4.East End 5. Camana Bay 6. Sunset House 7. Seven-Mile Beach 8. Smith Cove 9. George Town 10. North Side

Page 174 1) Grand Old House 2) Breakers 3) Crewe Road 4) East End
         5) Bodden Town 6) George Hicks Church, S Sound 7) Bodden Town

Page 176.   Bowling Alley, Hyperbaric Chamber
Baseball Diamond, Squash Club, Airbnb, Cricket Pitch, Athletics Stadium Museum, Theatre, Art Gallery

Page 178. 200 is the closest answer

Page 179. Jamaican 16.4%, Filipino 5.7%, British 2.4%, Indian 1.7

Page 179. The 3rd most popular name is Smith:
In the top ten: Scott, McLaughlin, Bush, and Thompson

Page 180. (Capacity in brackets -2020) Symphony of the Seas (7,600 inc. crew), Correctional Facility, Pennsylvania (8,811), Centre Court, Wimbledon (15,000), United Center, Chicago (23,500), Cambridge University, England (35,000), Adelaide Oval (53,000), Tottenham Hotspur, London (62,000)

CHAPTER ELEVEN

The Power of Nature

Tropical Storms

In the summer months, the water temperature in the northern hemisphere rises. This warm water might make it comfortable for holidaymakers to swim in the sea, but it also increases the risk of a very powerful weather phenomenon. In tropical regions, like between Africa and the Caribbean, the water gets warmer and the hot moist air rises and forms huge cloud systems. Some of these systems develop into tropical storms. As the world turns, these storm systems make their way west, across the Atlantic towards the Caribbean. If the conditions are right, they can develop into hurricanes. People in the Caribbean track the storms and hurricanes very carefully. If the storms start in the Atlantic, they may take more than a week to arrive at a Caribbean island. Other storm systems do not give such a warning. They simply pop up over the warm waters of the Caribbean itself - almost overnight and can be wreaking havoc on a nearby country the next day!

How fast does a hurricane move 'forward'?

It depends on its latitude. At Cayman-type latitudes of between 15°-25° North, a hurricane would typically travel at......

A) .... about 11 miles per hour (much slower than a turtle swims)

B) ... about 37 mph (the top speed of a dolphin)

C) ... about 70 mph (the top speed of a sailfish)

answers on page 198

Storm Categories

Meteorological experts rank storms in a certain order, based mainly on the speed of their maximum sustained winds. The list below is from the National Hurricane Center, Miami.

Hurricane Category 5	157 mph or higher
Hurricane Category 4	130-156 mph
Hurricane Category 3	111-129-mph
Hurricane Category 2	96-110 mph
Hurricane Category 1	74-95 mph
Tropical Storm	39-73 mph (34 to 63 knots)
Tropical Depression	less than 39 mph
Tropical Disturbance	

This statement by the National Hurricane Center describes the type of damage that may be expected by one of the hurricane categories mentioned above. Which one?

"Devastating damage will occur: Well-built framed homes may incur major damage or removal of roof decking and gable ends. Many trees will be snapped or uprooted, blocking numerous roads. Electricity and water will be unavailable for several days to weeks after the storm passes."

answers on page 198

Hurricanes and Tropical Storms from Cayman's Past

2022 September 26th Hurricane Ian This storm brushed past Cayman as a Category 1 Hurricane, about 65 miles to the west, causing little damage. However, it developed quickly afterwards, battering Cuba before going on to destroy parts of Florida. It made landfall in the Fort Myers/ Sanibel Island area as a Category 4, making thousands homeless and causing billions of dollars' worth of damage. Its 155 mph winds made it the fifth strongest hurricane to hit the US mainland. Cayman got off very lightly with this one.

2021 August 18th Tropical Storm Grace Everyone could see this storm approaching for several days. All the predictions showed it was on a direct course for Cayman, but it was projected not to turn into a hurricane until after it had passed. This turned out to be correct, but this 'mere' tropical storm hit Cayman directly and inflicted lots more damage than most people anticipated. Grace had sustained winds of 65 mph, with gusts of around 100 mph. It smashed docks, uprooted over a thousand trees, tore roofs off some vulnerable structures and flooded homes in West Bay and the Snug Harbour area, and broke several boats free from their moorings. Smith Cove was also a victim of Grace, with many of the trees there being uprooted. Restaurants that had already been suffering due to a lack of tourists were also badly damaged. Both Tukka locations sustained structural damage, the tree at Coconut Joe's came crashing down onto the outside deck space and the dock bar at the White House in Bodden Town was lifted by the sea and smashed on the beach in pieces. Although CUC did a great job of restoring electricity to most of the island on the day of the storm, some parts of the island were without power for a couple of days.

2020 October 6th - Hurricane Delta

This sneaky rascal was not supposed to develop into a hurricane until it reached the Yucatan Channel - the gap between Cuba and the Yucatan Peninsula. However, as it approached the South side of Cayman it intensified from a Tropical Storm to a Category 4 hurricane in just 30 hours! Fortunately, it strayed a little off course and stayed 100 miles away. What could have been a disaster only gave Cayman weather typical of a Nor'Wester.

2020 November 7th - Tropical Storm Eta

Cayman residents thought they had escaped this storm. It had travelled almost directly westward across the lower part of the Caribbean Sea and had hit South America as a major Hurricane, causing widespread damage and destruction. It was awful for thousands of people made homeless by flooding in Guatemala, Nicaragua and Honduras but surely this one had missed Cayman. But being 2020, this storm decided to do more damage and bounced off the mainland and aimed back towards Cayman. It passed within 30 miles of Grand Cayman as a Tropical Storm with winds of 60 mph. It brought with it very heavy rainfall, flooding areas of Savannah and Lower Valley. Some trees were uprooted, with a couple landing on parked cars. The pattern of damage to trees and utility poles in Savannah, splitting them in two, was interpreted by some that there may have been localised tornadoes!

2020 was a record-breaking year in terms of weather systems. Usually, a hurricane season, running from June 1st to through November 31st has a dozen or so named storms. In 2020, there were two named preseason storms in May and then enough storms to go through the entire 21-letter alphabet (there are five 5 letters that are not used) by September! By the end of the official hurricane season there had been 30 named storms, 13 hurricanes including 5 major ones (Category 3 or higher), 2 major hurricanes in November, over 40 billion dollars-worth of damage, tens of thousands of destroyed homes in Central America, and 12 storms had made landfall in the contiguous USA – breaking a record of 9, set in 1916.

2008 November 8th - Hurricane Paloma

The Hurricane came from South America and came very close to Grand Cayman as a major hurricane. It made landfall the following day on Little Cayman and Cayman Brac as a Category 4 hurricane, causing serious damage.

2004 September 12th - Hurricane Ivan

This beast passed within 15 or so miles to the south of Grand Cayman as a Category 5 hurricane! It had sustained winds of 160 miles per hour, with gusts of up to 160 mph. Wave heights were reported of between 20-30 feet. Its accompanying, huge, storm surges of 8-10 feet flooded the island – submerging large areas and demolishing buildings, causing damage costing almost 3 billion dollars. Grand Cayman suffered sustained winds of over 100 mph for over seven hours. About a quarter of homes were made uninhabitable, with roofs and walls missing or severely damaged.

A Cayman home destroyed by Hurricane Ivan

The deaths of two people were attributed to Hurricane Ivan, and hundreds more needed treatment for wounds and injuries.

Grand Cayman was without power, piped drinking water and sanitation for months. Schools were closed for several weeks. Thousands of people needed to be housed in shelters until houses were built.

Hurricane Ivan was record-breaking in terms of how long it stayed at high intensity. It managed to maintain 'at or above Category 4' for an amazing thirty-three 6-hour periods.

1998 October 25th - Hurricane Mitch

Hurricane Mitch is the second-deadliest Atlantic hurricane on record. It caused approximately 11,000 fatalities in Central America, with over 7,000 in Honduras alone, due to catastrophic flooding. Thankfully, the closest Mitch got to Cayman was 190 miles to the south (65 miles further away than predicted) so damage to the island was limited.

1988   September 13th - Hurricane Gilbert

Gilbert was the most intense Caribbean hurricane on record for decades and was only surpassed by Hurricane Wilma in 2015 and even now holds second place. It passed just 30 miles south of Grand Cayman as a Category 4. This hurricane killed 318 people in the Caribbean / Gulf of Mexico region and demolished 60,000 homes on the Yucatan Peninsula.

The 1932 Storm or Cuba Hurricane - November.

All three Cayman Islands were badly damaged by a slow-moving Category 5 hurricane that killed one person on Grand Cayman, 68 people on Cayman Brac and 40 more Caymanians at sea. This deadly storm has been featured in other chapters.

Twenty-one Names

The practice of naming storms began in the 1950s and evolved into the system we have today. For each letter used there are 3 boys' names and 3 girls' names, which alternate in a 6-year rotation. For example, names on the list beginning with A are currently:

Arthur (2020), Ana (2021), Alex (2022), Arlene (2023), Alberto (2024) and Andrea (2025). In 2026 it will revert to Arthur again.

It is difficult to find 6 pronounceable names for all 26 letters of the alphabet, so there are 5 letters that do not appear in the list.

a) Take an educated guess at which 5 letters are not used for hurricane names.

b) These famous people share their names with those of hurricanes on the 2021 tropical storm list. Can you identify them?

1. .... 2. .... 3. .... 4. ....

answers on page 198

Greek Letters

The contingency plan for naming storms, if there were more than 21 in a season, used to be to continue with the Greek alphabet. This system was only used twice. In 2005 six Greek letters were used, and the system was kept in place. However, in the 2020 season tropical storms were so rampant that nine letters from the Greek alphabet had to be used - which caused a lot of confusion. Not everyone is familiar with the Greek alphabet and, looking at the 'English' initial letters of the first few Greek words, it is easy to see why people became bewildered:

A, B, G, D, E, Z, E, T, I

The 6th, 7th and 8th letters also sound the same, and in 2020 people were getting them mixed up. Also, some people assumed that Zeta was the last letter in the alphabet and wondered which alphabet would be used next. As confusion can cost lives, the World Meteorological Organisation announced that, beginning with the 2021 season, there would be a back-up list of 21 names to be used - starting with Adria, Braylen, and Caridad. Let us hope this is rarely needed.

a) How many of the first nine Greek letters can you name?

alpha_____   b_____   g_____   d_____

e_____   z_____   e_____   t_____

i_____

b) What is the *last* letter of the Greek alphabet?   _____

c) What is the Greek name for the letter 'O'   _____

(hint: most people heard of it for the first time during the Covid pandemic.)

answers on page 198

Retired Names

Some hurricanes cause so much loss of life and destruction that no one wants to hear their names ever again. These storm names are 'retired' by the World Meteorological Association. Such is the devastation caused by hurricanes that several names have been discarded each decade. The table below shows how many names have been retired in each of the last few decades. The 1970s was the first time that men's names were included in the list.

Decade	Number of Names Retired	Most Deadly Hurricane of the Decade
1970s	9	Fifi (Jamaica) 8,200 deaths
1980s	7	Gilbert (Jamaica, Venezuela, Central America, Hispaniola, Mexico) 318 deaths
1990s	15	Mitch (Central America, Yucatán Peninsula, South Florida) over 11,000 deaths
2000s	**24**	Jeanne (The Caribbean, Eastern United States) 3,035 deaths
2010s	16	Maria (Lesser Antilles, Puerto Rico) 3,057 deaths
2020s *(up to December 2021)	3	Eta (Central America, Cuba, Southeastern United States) 211 deaths*

Which of the names in the 'Cayman Hurricanes' section fit the 'too awful to ever hear of again' criteria and have been retired?

Ivan   Gilbert   Mitch   Paloma

answers on page 198

2017   Three Hurricanes at a Time

When it comes to hurricanes, some years are more worrying than others. The 2020 season kept everyone on their toes, throughout the Caribbean. Although there were fewer storms in 2017, compared to 2020, it was still a very active season. There were a few close calls for Cayman and plenty of activity to keep our collective eyes on. In one week, in early September, there were three hurricanes at one time bearing down on the Caribbean.

This satellite image (below), taken by the U.S. National Oceanic and Atmospheric Administration, captures Hurricane Katia (left) making landfall over Mexico, Hurricane Irma over Cuba, and Hurricane Jose building up to peak intensity.

U.S. National Oceanic and Atmospheric Administration (public domain)
Hurricanes Katia, Irma and Jose: Sept 8th, 2017

The 2017 season was the costliest on record, with damage estimated at almost 300 billion dollars! Harvey, Irma, and Maria did the most damage, while Hurricane Nate became Costa Rica's most destructive natural disaster in the country's history. In all, at least 3,364 people had been killed by the storms across the region. The names Harvey, Irma, Maria and Nate were all retired from the WMA's list.

Earthquakes

The Caribbean gets its fair share of earthquakes. The islands along the Eastern Caribbean are along a subduction zone, which explains why there are so many volcanoes. The volcanoes cause some (volcanic) earthquakes, and the rest are tectonic earthquakes – caused by the denser, North American Plate sliding under the lighter, Caribbean Plate. This action causes upward thrusts as one block of crust slides over the other, so they are called thrust, or reverse faults and can cause massive tsunami waves.

Puerto Rico lies at a subduction zone, with a trough over 27,000 feet deep to the north and a trough to the south over 15,000 feet deep. In December 2019 and January 2020, Puerto Rico was hit by an earthquake swarm including six with a magnitude of 5 or higher – the strongest being magnitude 6.4.

The Greater Antilles has strike-slip faults where one plate slides horizontally against the next. Although this action provides far less of a threat of tsunamis, it can still cause devastating earthquakes. In 2010, more than a quarter of a million people were killed by a magnitude 7.0 earthquake in Haiti, with many more injured. Half a million people were made homeless, and four thousand schools were destroyed. Countries around the world raised massive amounts of money to provide aid for the country; a country that was already desperately poor before the earthquake struck.

In 1907, a 6.5 magnitude earthquake struck Jamaica and damaged or destroyed every building in the capital, Kingston. Over 1,000 people were killed by the quake and the subsequent fires that engulfed parts of the city. It was followed shortly after by a 2-metre tsunami. This was not Jamaica's first killer earthquake. You may remember one being mentioned in the days of piracy. Port Royal, a pirate haven, was struck in 1692 causing most of the city to sink below sea level. Two thousand people died, either directly in the earthquake or from their injuries and disease in the following days.

Tsunamis

Most tsunamis are caused by undersea earthquakes at tectonic plate boundaries. The bigger ones are caused when one plate slides under the other, displacing the water above it. That event then launches waves, perhaps just 1-2 feet high, that travel at 500 miles per hour away from the earthquake. The waves can retain their energy for thousands of miles and as they approach sloping seabeds near land, they slow down and pile upwards. The leading trough of the wave can draw all the water out of a harbour or bay, which is a sure sign of what is coming next. If this happens everyone should run inland and get as high as they can because within a few minutes the crest of the wave will form a tsunami (Japanese for harbour wave). The enlarged wave will rush into the bay at a height much greater than the sea was previously and inundate the whole area. Water is immensely powerful, and incoming waves will be carrying all the debris of everything that they have knocked down and destroyed in their path.

Eighty percent of tsunamis happen within the Pacific Ocean's 'Ring of Fire', so they are much less of a threat to islands in the Caribbean. Also, Cayman's steep drop-offs and lack of continental shelf make conditions less than favourable for a tsunami to build up and be devastating. Also, the plate boundaries in the vicinity of Cayman are the strike-slip type, sliding against each other horizontally, so they do not generate the huge displacement of water that is caused by the vertical, subduction-zone actions.

The 7.7 magnitude earthquake northeast of Cayman in 2020 initiated a flow of water, but there was no noticeable tsunami as it went past Cayman. A wave of less than two feet was reported.

Answer these questions to find out what you know about tsunamis.

1) If you lived on an island, and an earthquake 200 miles away sent a tsunami wave in your direction, how long would it take to reach you?

a) about half an hour   b) 3 hours   c) 4 hours   d) 9 hours

2)   If you were a half mile out at sea in a boat and you heard that a tsunami was heading in your direction. What should you do?

a) sail or power the boat back to a mooring or dock and secure it firmly

b) sail or power the boat back to a mooring or dock and secure it firmly – then run inland and get into a tall, strong building

c) sail or power the boat a little further out to sea and enjoy the sunshine

answers on page 198

The 2020 Cayman Earthquake

The Cayman Islands, generally, do not suffer from earthquakes. However, on January 28th, 2020, a powerful magnitude 7.7 quake occurred on the Oriente fault zone that runs along the Cayman trench towards Cuba's south-east tip. Although it was reported as being a 'Jamaica' earthquake, being 130 km from Montego Bay, it was considerably closer to Cayman – 108 km from Spot Bay, Little Cayman.

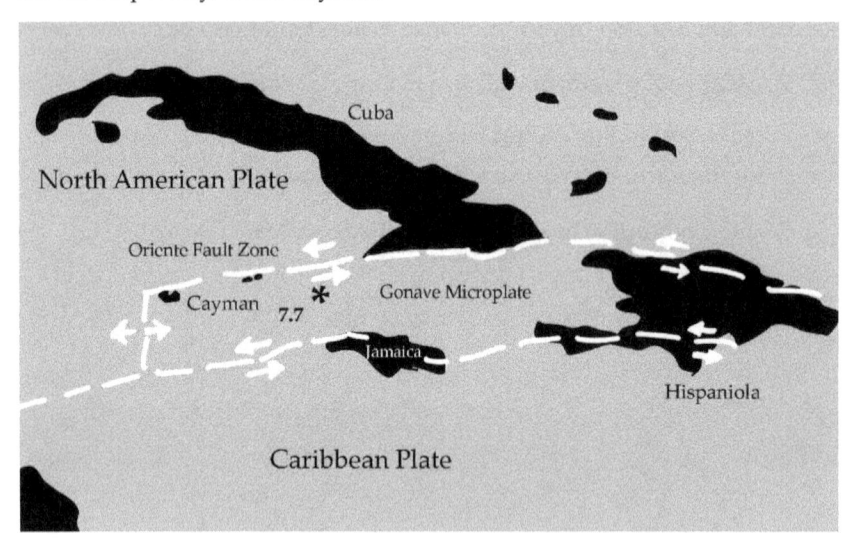

The 7.7 magnitude 'Jamaica Earthquake' of 2020

Thankfully, there were no reported injuries and very little damage in Cayman. However, the earthquake did cause several sinkholes to emerge across Grand Cayman. As the earthquake was happening there was a very noticeable side-to-side motion – standing still or walking felt like being on a rope-bridge, swaying over a ravine. One would expect such movement on a rope-bridge but on the flat, concrete pavement underfoot it was disconcerting for the solid ground to be acting that way!

For anyone who was close enough to observe the water in a swimming pool, the rocking motion of the water in the pool was most impressive, first splashing up and out of one side, and then moving across and splashing out of the other.

Here is a brief list of some infamous earthquakes, in order of moment magnitude. **Between which two does the Cayman/Jamaica earthquake of 2020 belong?**

	Where	When	Damage	Deaths
A	**Indian Ocean**	Boxing Day 2004	Massive destruction affecting many countries	227,898 in 14 countries
B	**San Francisco**	1906	80% of city destroyed	over 3,000
C	**Kashmir**	2005	Massive destruction to buildings and infrastructure	around 100,000 including 19,000 schoolchildren
D	**Canterbury, New Zealand**	2010	40 billion dollars-worth of damage	185
E	**Haiti**	2010	Utter devastation 250,000 homes destroyed	over 160,000

answers on page 198

Answers for Chapter 11

Page 183. (A) About 11 mph, though they can move even more slowly or stall altogether.

Page 184. The statement describes a Category 3 hurricane.

Page 189. a) Q U X Y Z are not used

b) Teresa, Bill, Fred, Henri

Page 191.   a) beta, gamma, delta, epsilon, zeta, eta, theta, iota, kappa

b) omega

c) omicron

Page 191 **All** of those names have been retired because their associated storms caused too much devastation and/or loss of life.

Page 195. 1. (a) About half an hour   2. (c) Stay at sea. The wave will just bob your boat up a little as it passes beneath

Page 1957 Between B and C   Kashmir (2005) and San Francisco (1906)

Earthquake	Moment magnitude
Indian Ocean	9.1
San Francisco	7.9
Cayman/Jamaica	**7.7**
Kashmir	7.6
New Zealand	7.1
Haiti	7.0

CHAPTER TWELVE

Pandemics in History

Pandemics, Epidemics, Endemics, Outbreaks and Plagues

First, it would be good to clear up the meaning of each of these terms as they are sometimes a cause of confusion. If you can't tell the difference between a paramedic and a pandemic, here's your chance to learn.

Diseases can be **endemic** to a particular place - like you might find a local dish, animal, or plant that is an *endemic* species. Malaria is endemic to parts of Africa. It lives there and stays there, but it usually does not spread far, and if the numbers stay under control, it retains its status as simply an endemic disease.

An **outbreak** is when the number of cases suddenly rises beyond what is usual. This might be caused by any number of factors, such as by a leak of toxins into a water supply, unsafe food, environmental factors, or perhaps a tourist bringing in a disease from his native country and infecting locals. Outbreaks tend to be limited in location or geographic area, such as near the town's reservoir, the public park where people bought the contaminated food, or the village downwind from the leaking chemical plant.

An **epidemic** is like an outbreak that has got out of control. It may have started as an outbreak, but it has quickly escalated, with larger numbers of people affected and the disease spreading further. The number of victims needed for each definition may vary from country to country, but an epidemic is always a larger scale event than an outbreak.

A **pandemic** is the big one. It ominously uses the prefix *pan,* which is from the Greek for *all* or *everyone* or *involving all members.* When diseases spread and cross into several countries, and even continents, they hit the big time and become pandemics.

On January 1st, 2020, the World Health Organisation (WHO) identified an outbreak of pneumonia cases connected to a novel coronavirus. Three weeks later there was evidence of human-to-human transmission in Wuhan. Before January even ended, WHO announced on the 30th that the outbreak constituted a Public Health Emergency of International Concern (PHEIC). On March 11th, 2020, WHO declared to the world that COVID-19 should be categorised as a pandemic. By then, there had been over 118,000 cases in well over 100 countries.

Surely that covers all the definitions, so what is a plague? Plague is a specific disease caused by the bacteria Yersinia pestis, transmitted by the bites from the fleas on rats and other small mammals. Humans can also be infected through contact with infected bodily fluids and by inhaling infected respiratory droplets.

It is possible to have a plague outbreak, a plague epidemic and even a plague pandemic, such as the Black Death – which might be named the bubonic pandemic if it were to happen today.

The Black Death (1346-1353)

The Black Death, or Bubonic Plague killed between 75 million and **200 million people** throughout Europe, Africa, and Asia, between 1346 and 1353. This coincided with movement along the commercial route known as the Silk Road – that connected Asia with Europe and Africa. Rats that lived aboard the ships coming from Asia carried fleas, which in turn, harboured the plague bacterium. The rats spread into densely packed urban areas around the ports when ships docked. Half of all Europeans were killed within seven years and overall, maybe as many as two-thirds of the European population was wiped out.

Symptoms of bubonic plague are swollen lymph nodes (buboes), which can become as large as eggs. Many victims would develop gangrene, a blackening of body tissue – hence the name 'black death'. If bubonic plague spreads to the lungs it can cause pneumonic plague which can very quickly become fatal. It is treated, today, by antibiotics – but in the fourteenth century there was little hope of survival.

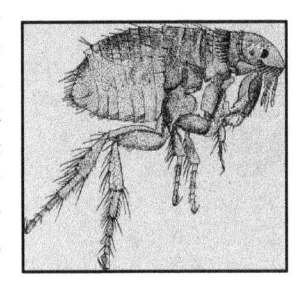

The spread of the bubonic plague has been attributed to fleas carried by rats.

There have been two other great pandemics of plague.

The Justinian Plague (541)

This one started in Constantinople and raged, in waves for 225 years, claiming millions of lives.

The Third Plague Pandemic - Hong Kong Plague (1894)

Yersinia pestis struck again, starting in the Yunnan province of China, and travelling the world until the 1950s It claimed around **15 million lives** – mainly in China and India, but as far afield as South Africa and San Francisco. It was during this plague that science found the bacterium responsible for the disease and understood the role that fleas played in its transmission.

Other notable plagues that did not become pandemics were the Italian Plague (1629-1631), the Great Plague of London (1665-1666), and the Great Plague of Marseille (1720-1722) - all in major trading and shipping centres.

The Influenza Pandemic (1918)

Twenty to **50 million people** died from influenza at the end of the first world war, between 1918-1920. It infected a third of the world's population - killing 10%-20% of those that it infected. There were 25 million deaths in the first 25 weeks alone. It was unusual, in that it tended to kill the stronger, healthier people rather than the elderly or people with weakened immune systems. Influenza also killed on a global scale, including in places as remote as the Arctic Circle, and the Pacific islands.

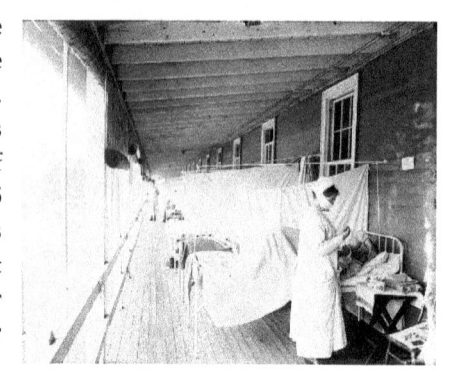

Influenza ward at Walter Reed Hospital, Washington D.C. during the 1918 flu pandemic.

The World Health Organisation estimates that between 290,000 and 650,000 people die every year from flu, worldwide. Complications can arise because the virus can cause, among other things, rapid respiratory failure and/or viral or bacterial pneumonia. Being vaccinated provides some protection from flu, where vaccines are available.

HIV/AIDS Pandemic

What we now know as HIV is closely related to a virus found in simian monkeys, chimpanzees, and gorillas in parts of Africa - simian immunodeficiency virus (SIV). Some strains of SIV began in Cameroon, and others began in the Belgian Congo - now known as the Democratic Republic of Congo. Scientists believe that the virus crossed over from monkeys and non-human apes to one that affected humans in the late 1800s and early 20th century. One way it may have done so is through the blood of animals being passed to the bush hunter, either at some part of the hunt or in the unhygienic butchery of the animals.

In the Scramble for Africa, the Congo was colonised by the Belgians, and Léopoldville (modern Kinshasa), became a thriving city – with one million people passing through it every year. With so many men working away from home there was an upsurge in promiscuous sexual activity and prostitution - leading to genital ulcer diseases (GUD), - which made ideal conditions for the transmission of the ancestral version of today's HIV.

Another factor that probably helped 'HIV' spread was the large number of unsterile injections that took place at the time. These were administered to either vaccinate against smallpox, or to deliver antibiotics in the 1950s to combat sleeping sickness. Unfortunately, traces of the infected blood of people in the cities, who were contaminated by the SIV from the bushmeat, and/or GUDs from their promiscuity, was passed on to others by the reusing of syringes and needles by health workers. It is estimated that 2,000 people had HIV in the 1960s in Africa, which is a relatively small number – so it is interesting to discover how it became a pandemic.

The long incubation period was a factor in the success of the spread of AIDS. When a virus can remain undetected for a long time, its hosts can unwittingly transmit the disease to more people.

In the early 1970s there was a 'junkie flu' going around in some American cities, and deaths from pneumonia complications seemed to be connected to intravenous drug use. By 1977 in New York City, these same sub-groups of people were beginning to die from the severity of the diseases, but as these were often homeless people, and had only scant access to healthcare, their deaths did not hit the headlines. There were also massive cuts to the health services that would have supported heroin users, such as methadone clinics, which made the problem worse.

Next, the slow-acting virus, and the devastating effect it had on the immune systems of those it infected, became associated with gay men. They tended to have many sexual partners, and anal intercourse provided ideal conditions for transmission of the virus. A report of cases amongst men in Southern California was published in June 1982, and the term GRIDs (Gay-related immune-deficiency) was suggested as a name for the syndrome. However, in August that year, when the CDC understood that, taken as a whole, only half the victims of the disease were homosexual men, they coined the term Acquired Immune Deficiency Syndrome (AIDS). The virus responsible for AIDS was isolated the following year, and after several teams also arrived at the same cause, it took on the name Human Immunodeficiency Virus (HIV), in 1986.

The World Health Organisation (WHO) classified HIV/AIDS as a pandemic in 1981, before it even had a name or known cause. Over the next fifteen years the number of cases and subsequent deaths was alarming as science raced to find a medical treatment. According to a report by WHO and UNAIDS in 1998 about statistics from the preceding year, there were 2.3 million deaths in 1997, from 5.8 million cases – with over 30 million people living with AIDS. This was the peak of the pandemic, but around 2 million deaths occurred in each of the next ten years.

To date, by 2022, AIDS has caused over **36 million deaths**, and is ongoing, particularly in parts of Africa. Where modern treatments are available, contracting HIV no longer means a death sentence. However, where modern medicines are not available, patients may expect to live for just eleven more years.

SARS-Cov-2 Pandemic (2020 - present)

Severe Acute Respiratory Syndrome - Coronavirus 2, hit the world in 2019. Sars-Cov-2 was the name of the virus causing the disease, as it was related to the SARS virus of 2003. Covid-19 was the name given by the WHO to the *disease* caused by the SARS virus, with the suffix 19 indicating the year of its first recorded case.

The first known case of Covid-19 was identified in Wuhan, China, in December 2019. The disease spread worldwide quickly, with the number of cases doubling every 2-3 days. By March 2020 there were 800,000 confirmed cases and 40,000 deaths. In about twenty percent of cases, patients suffered mild to moderate symptoms, but in 14% of cases victims developed severe symptoms such as dyspnoea or hypoxia. The most severe 5% of cases developed critical symptoms, such as respiratory failure or multi-organ dysfunction. Many of these sufferers could not be saved.

With world travel so easy in 2020, it was easy for the virus to spread from country to country. Fortunately, information was able to spread even faster, and as other nations became aware of the virus, borders started to close, and the world went into various forms of isolation. Australia, for instance, closed its borders to international travellers for almost two years, from March 2020 to February 2022.

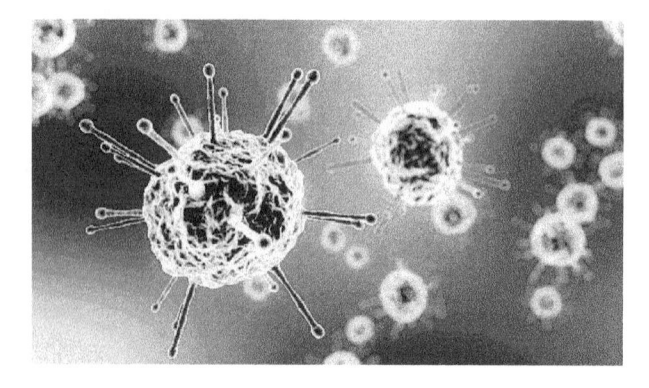

The Sars- CoV-2 virus

Despite non-medical interventions, such as border closures, school closures, the wearing of masks, and social distancing, deaths from Covid-19 grew at an alarming rate. By September 2020, over one million deaths were reported. The 5 million fatalities mark was passed in October 2021. Bear in mind, this was with access to 21st century medicine and life-saving equipment, such as ventilators.

Isolating people from their communities was necessary at first but unsustainable as a permanent solution. Essential work that keeps cities alive, such as power services, water supply, sanitation, and the supply of food and goods to supermarkets must continue. Not everyone could work from home. People needed to earn a living or face bankruptcy and foreclosures, and some normality had to be restored. The only hope was that science could somehow develop a vaccine against the virus – in a matter of months, rather than decades. Amazingly, a vaccine was developed, and began to be administered, at first in the UK, from December 2020, with the USA quickly following suit. The world would soon be able to embrace a new kind of normal. In June 2022, Bloomberg reported that 12 billion vaccination shots had been given worldwide – a remarkable achievement.

Just prior to that, in May 2022, the World Health Organisation announced some sobering news. Most people at that time believed that there had been around 6 million Covid related deaths, but the report by WHO had looked at data a different way. It had looked at the 'excess deaths' - fatalities that had occurred above the number that would have happened without Covid. WHO concluded that it was more accurate to attribute almost **15 million deaths** to Covid-19 in the years 2020 and 2021.

Vaccination

Immunity from a disease is the ultimate form of defence. Vaccinations have helped man eradicate several diseases that used to be commonplace for our ancestors, including some lethal ones. Here is a brief history of vaccinations, from Cowpox to SARS-CoV-2

Inoculations, Variolations and Vaccinations

Edward Jenner, the country doctor from Gloucestershire, England, is often hailed as the person whose discoveries and work has saved more lives than the contributions of any other person throughout man's history. This may be an overstatement – as it is rare that any one person contributes so much in isolation, but he and other people mentioned here deserve a great deal of credit for the eradication of smallpox and the introduction of immunising people against diseases.

After studying medicine in London, Jenner moved back to his hometown, Berkeley, and set up as a medical practitioner and surgeon. It was there that he made his observations about cowpox, namely that milkmaids who contracted the mildly irritating cowpox somehow had protection from the vicious, lethal disease smallpox. The risk of death after being infected by smallpox was 30%, or even worse with some variants, and the prognosis for babies was worse than for adults. One third of all cases of blindness in 18th century Europe may have been attributable to smallpox. In the 20th century alone, it is estimated that 300 million people died from the disease.

Inoculate is a general term that typically means to implant into a person (or animal or plant) an antigen (such as a toxin, a virus, or other undesirable substance) that then induces an immune response in the host, so that it makes antibodies that are then capable of defending the person against a serious disease. Before inoculation by vaccination, a term taken from the Latin (vacca) for cows, there was inoculation by variolation. There are records of variolation in China as long ago as the 15th century.

By the 1700s variolation was being used in India, Africa, the Ottoman Empire and more tentatively in England in the mid-18th century. Lady Montagu of London survived smallpox in Turkey, in 1715, and afterward had her 5-year-old son variolated to protect him from the disease. When she returned to England, the procedure was used successfully on her four-year-old daughter, but despite Lady Montagu's status and efforts to make variolation accessible to people in England, the practice did not become popular as it was seen as Oriental, irreligious and 'a fad of ignorant women.'

Variolation did arouse some interest. In the same year as Lady Montagu's return to England, 1721, it was tested on six condemned prisoners. They were later exposed to smallpox and survived - and released for their participation in the risky experiment.

The fatality rate of people contracting smallpox at that time was between 14-30% The option was to find a person with a mild form of the infection, extract matter from their pustules and scrape it across an open wound made on the arm or leg of a healthy individual. People who were variolated in this way had a reduced risk of dying from smallpox – as low as 1 or 2%. This was still not without risk. Several notable people died from this procedure, including the son of King George III. Unfortunately, variolation was the only way one could be inoculated against diseases, until vaccination came along.

The main proponent of vaccinations was Edward Jenner, as already stated. In his late forties, and with many years in medicine behind him, he performed an extraordinary experiment on an eight-year-old boy. In 1796, Jenner took cowpox matter from an infected dairymaid and put it into two small cuts he had made on the arm of James Phipps, the son of his gardener. The boy had a mild fever about one week later but was well again within two days. Then came the dangerous part. Six weeks later, Jenner inoculated the boy with smallpox - which could have killed him. Medical ethics were not as developed back then, obviously. The smallpox had no harmful effect on him, which made Jenner conclude that the boy now had immunity. To further test his theory, Jenner proceeded to infect the boy twenty more times. The boy still did not die, thankfully, and Jenner published his conclusions. Jenner's findings were not readily accepted in the medical community and at times he was ridiculed, but by 1840 vaccination was the inoculation of choice in England, and variolation was banned.

Ultimately, if a virus has no hosts, it has no way of surviving. Over the next 140 years from 1840, the practice of vaccinating the public against all kinds of diseases saw some of them disappear, at least within some geographical boundaries. For instance, there has not been a case of polio originating in the United States since 1979.

Smallpox was such a threat to humans that it was not sufficient to eradicate this malevolent virus from one country, or even a continent, as there would always be a chance of it making a comeback. It was, therefore, vital that the world united completely against it. To the world's credit, a concerted attack on smallpox, through vaccination, began shortly after World War II. In 1980 the World Health Organisation was able to announce, "Smallpox is Dead!"

Vaccine Questions

1. Why was SARS-2 or Covid-19 referred to as a 'novel coronavirus'?

2. In most countries, at least 90% of infants are given a vaccination to protect them against 3 nasty diseases. Which three?

3. What was the outcome of an article, published in a British medical journal in 1998, suggesting a link between the childhood vaccine mentioned in question 2, above, and autism?

4. Here are some scientific (genus) names of animals. What are they?

a) canis   b) panthera   c) homo   d) equus   e) bos   f) vulpes   g) ursus

answers on page 212

Answers for Chapter 12

Page 211

1. Corona means crown. Under the microscope, parts of some viruses seem to have a crown-like appearance – spikes coming from the surface. This was noticed in the 1960s in the common cold viruses. There are around 40 coronaviruses. In 2019, a new one emerged (SARS CoV-19). Novel means new.

2. MMR – Measles, mumps, and rubella (German measles).

3. Thousands of people in the UK, America, and other countries began withdrawing their children from the MMR vaccine programme, putting them at great risk. Many will have suffered needlessly. According to WHO estimates, 140,000 people died worldwide in 2018 from measles – an entirely preventable disease. There was no science behind the doctor's claim, as has been demonstrated by countless studies, and he had his licence to practise medicine taken away.

4. a) wolf (includes dogs) b) panther (includes lions and tigers)

   c) human d) horse (includes zebra and donkeys) e) cow f) fox g) bear

CHAPTER THIRTEEN

The Coronavirus Pandemic in Cayman

We will all remember 2020. What a year! The amazing part is, that although it may have seemed bad at the time, most of the rest of the world had an even worse experience and we got off lightly in Cayman. As the COVID-19 pandemic was looming unseen beyond the horizon, a couple of other events heralded in the New Year in Cayman that made us begin to believe that even in Cayman, our safety was not 100% assured.

On January 28th, 2020, a violent earthquake shook the Cayman Islands from side-to-side. Considering that the earthquake was magnitude 7.7, Cayman came out of it relatively unscathed. But even as we huddled together at assembly points, experts at the World Health Organisation were getting ready to announce that there was a Public Health Emergency of International Concern, (PHEIC).

On February 29th, the cruise ship Costa Luminosa, that had been turned away by Jamaica as a COVID-19 precaution, had been given permission to stop in Cayman so that a passenger who was suffering from a critical cardiac issue could be rushed to hospital. The news hit the headlines, but there was little more reported about it over the next few days, so it receded into the background as a new event gripped everyone's attention.

On March 8th, the dump, also known as 'Mount Trashmore', caught on fire. This started small, but soon grew out of control, and needed the attendance of firefighters for almost a week - as every time it seemed to have died down, it came back to life again. It forced one nearby school to close, and a few people were treated at hospital for respiratory problems. From what the World Health Organisation (WHO) was discovering, the whole world might soon have difficulty breathing.

The Lockdown for COVID-19

On March 14th, just three days after WHO had declared the COVID-19 outbreak a global pandemic, the Italian cruise ship passenger who had been transferred from the Costa Luminosa to the hospital, died of his condition. It was confirmed that he had tested positive for the coronavirus. The severity of the situation struck a chord with Cayman's leaders, and the awareness of the country's vulnerability to infection by visitors became abundantly clear. Two days later, the ports were closed to cruise ships and private yachts. Immediately, travel restrictions were put in place for people coming from hotspot areas, but this was recognized as insufficient, so by 22nd March the Cayman border was completely closed, with the only exceptions being cargo, air ambulances, and repatriation flights.

Children and teachers attending school on Friday 13th March were instructed to gather whatever they might need in case schools became closed for a while, and that turned out to be the final school day of the year. Schools did not resume after the weekend, and distance-learning through computers was the new normal practice until after the summer vacation.

With only a few hiccups at the beginning of the lockdown, the isolation of the entire population of Cayman was a very efficient and effective affair. Curfews were in place, keeping people in their homes on Sundays and after 7:00pm. People were permitted to shop for essential supplies at supermarkets, pharmacies, and gas stations, but to limit numbers out at any one time, they were divided into surnames A-K and L-Z. Food could be delivered from restaurants to homes, or people could pick it up kerbside. Daily exercise was also allowed, so it would be common to see people out walking.

Gathering in public places was not allowed, though. At first, people were allowed to exercise on the beach – which was very pleasant. Unfortunately, due to a minority abusing this privilege so that they could party, this was soon stopped. It also was against the rules to congregate at pools, so strata/condominium pools were all off-limits.

The must-watch programme of the day was the CI Government's YouTube briefing, scheduled to begin at 2:00 pm - though it seldom did. Here, we got a daily dose of the state of play on the islands. His Excellency the Governor, Martin Roper, put forward how the UK would be assisting in any way possible. Premier McLaughlin read out the statistics related to cases and deaths around the world and followed this by explaining the reasoning behind any decisions that were being made, relating to border closures, curfews, and the like. Chief Inspector Byrne laid down the ever-changing laws and orders, and the penalties for breaking them. He also indicated the number of incidents and breaches of curfews that had occurred, and what had happened to the culprits. The other main player in the developing drama was Chief medical officer Dr. John Lee. He soon became everyone's favourite, with his calm demeanour, acting as a knowledgeable and trustworthy spokesman of science.

Having a lockdown kept everyone safe, but there was an obvious economic crisis looming. Many Caymanians depend on tourism for their livelihood and there was constant pressure on the government to consider easing border restrictions. The premier, guided by Chief Medical Officer Dr. John Lee, was extremely sensible throughout, placing the emphasis on safety. He often responded to those advocating loosening restrictions by pointing out that dead customers would not be able to buy anything.

The Cayman Islands makes its money through indirect taxation. It has three main revenue streams. The obvious one is tourism, but Cayman is also a major offshore financial centre, which was still able to operate with bankers and accountants working from home. The third source of income is construction. The CI Government collects duty on land and real estate sales, and further duty on all the imported building materials. Also, employers need to pay for work-permits for non-Caymanian workers. If the country could get to a point where there was no community spread of the virus, it could restart construction, and even get the whole local economy going again, including reopening bars, shops, and restaurants. There just would be no overseas tourists.

The initial target was to have four weeks with no cases of COVID-19, to go safely beyond the incubation stage and have a margin of error. The government tested all likely carriers frequently, and several days would go by with no new cases. Then, frustratingly, just one or two people would test positive. Sometimes, we knew that the positive case had been a family member of someone who was infected, but sometimes they were not, which meant there was a real danger lurking in the community. We waited, tantalised, and locked down for weeks, until finally the virus had run out of new hosts and disappeared.

On the 12th of August, it was announced that PAHO (Pan-American Health Organization) had declared Cayman COVID-free. By then, Cayman had conducted almost 32,000 tests, recording only 203 positive cases – with most of those being in isolation at the time. It had been one month since the last recorded positive case.

In the spring of 2020, Cayman established an air-bridge between London and Cayman, and occasionally between the USA or Canada and Cayman. This was used for returning residents and for the transportation of PPE, ventilators, and testing kits. Many students had returned home for the summer, and some non-Caymanian workers had used the outgoing flights, which could only be booked through the government, to travel home. Incoming travellers were obviously the main threat to the island, and these were generally placed in quarantine facilities for two weeks and released after testing negative.

Cayman was operating as normal during the summer, with residents allowed to go to bars, restaurants, and shops without masks. Visiting beaches and pools was permissible. Hotels and condos benefited from people needing a holiday by offering staycations, which were very popular. Although there would usually be a few people tucked away in quarantine, isolated away from everyone else, everyday life on the island had resumed.

The New Normal

Amazingly, while the rest of the world suffered from lockdowns and massive numbers of COVID-19 cases and related deaths, from July to the end of 2021 life in Cayman was 'normal' - except for the obvious lack of tourists. Some other changes were more subtle.

A lot of people, especially in the financial sector, now worked from home for much of the time. There had been no lack of productivity during lock-down and many realised that they could have a better quality of life with less commuting time.

The hotels on 7-Mile Beach, which employed hundreds of staff and had huge overheads, were virtually empty, except for staycation guests. Others who depended on tourism, like taxi-drivers, tour operators, people connected with the watersports and the dive industry, and the owners and staff of the George Town shops and bars that depended on cruise ship passengers, all saw their livelihoods – and presumably, their savings, disappear. People adapted as best they could, but there was real suffering in many quarters – in a country known for its affluence. The government provided some temporary financial aid for around 3,000 workers, in the form of a stipend of CI$1500 per month, known as the Displaced Tourism Employees Stipend Programme. In fact, this temporary government stipend was still being paid up to June 2022, having cost over $105 million in total. Unfortunately, there was some abuse of the honesty-based stipend system. Eventually, some recipients went back to work but still claimed the stipend. It was also discovered that four prison inmates were receiving the monthly stipend, despite being incarcerated and unavailable to work.

School children returned to school in September. There was no need for masks, 'bubbles', or part-time schooling, as in some countries. A few older students, who may have left to study abroad had there been no pandemic, remained. A few families who may have been due to leave, decided not to move from a Covid-free island to a country rife with disease, so they stayed.

School-life continued, complete with assemblies, Christmas pageants, and graduation celebrations - up to a limit of 500 attendees. The biggest difference at schools was that it was likely that final exams, including ones required to earn a place at universities, would probably not take place at the end of the school year. This had happened in summer 2020, when UK exam boards issued grades based on teacher assessments.

Breaches

From summer 2020 to the end of the year, Cayman was ticking over, with the financial and construction industries working well there was freedom of movement inside the country. Bars and restaurants were open, and local commerce was helping to keep most people afloat. However, there needed to be *some* movement of people, and with that, potentially the virus, across the border. Students living in the UK, US and Canada and some other travellers, needed to return to Cayman from time to time, particularly for the summer and Christmas vacations. Many 'snow-birds' who typically spend a few months escaping the cold weather back home, wanted to return to their part-time homes and get away from something much more sinister than winter chills. Also, Cayman was being advertised as a safe place to stay, for anyone who could work remotely. All these people could try to find a coveted spot on a rare flight to Cayman and head to the islands. However, any one of them could potentially carry the virus and send the whole island into lockdown again, or much worse, spread the disease and cause deaths. By December, only one resident, in addition to the cruise-ship passenger, had died from COVID-19, and even that was one too many. Allowing people into Cayman had to be done, as it had been thus far, with great care and consideration.

From day one, the CI Government had put in place quarantine and isolation measures for returning Caymanians and residents. Now that incoming flights, which were very limited in number and were only bookable through the government, were going to allow people into the country more frequently, a system was introduced whereby incoming travellers were fitted with an electronic tagging device. These people then had to quarantine at a government facility or an approved, suitably secure private residence for fourteen days. To support this, there was a deterrent of a fine of $10,000 and/or a prison sentence of up to six months. Anybody thinking that these measures would make everyone comply would be mistaken.

First to breach quarantine was a couple visiting from Canada. Dr. Pascal Terjanian and his partner Christina Gurunian both pleaded guilty to breaches of quarantine during their stay at their condo at Regal Beach. It was revealed in court that they had been seen on CCTV walking around the complex, walking on the beach, and swimming in the sea. It is also reported that they visited a nearby hotel that was open to the public. The couple managed to do all this by tampering with their monitoring wristbands. It is not clear why they were allowed into the country for a 14-day visit, as this would have indicated that their whole stay would have been under quarantine.

Similarly, given that all visitors needed to self-isolate for two weeks, it may have been a good idea to question why Skylar Mack, an 18-year-old from Georgia, was visiting Cayman for a short stay during a pandemic. She arrived on November 27th, and the competition in which her boyfriend, local professional jet ski rider Vanjae 'VJ' Ramgeet, was taking part, was just two days later. Upon arrival in Cayman Miss Mack was fitted with a geo-fencing bracelet, but she complained the next day that it was too tight. Health workers attended the teenager in isolation and obligingly loosened it for her. On the day of the event, the 29th, the pre-med student managed to slip off the electronic device and attended the National Jet Ski Race to watch her boyfriend compete. There, Miss Mack, herself the daughter of an international jet ski rider, spent several hours mixing with people - before being arrested. She and her boyfriend were sentenced, after one appeal for a stricter sentence by the government and then an appeal by defence counsels for a more lenient one, to two months imprisonment. The couple each received fines and VJ Ramgeet was stripped of his competition winnings by the Watersports Association. He also lost a sponsorship deal.

There was one other notable breach in 2020, when a local Caymanian teenager, who had returned home from school in the USA, broke out of isolation – twice. The 19-year-old male was initially staying in a secure government facility. After he escaped from there, he was taken to his family home. According to the Medical Officer of Health there were unique considerations to be made in this case and isolating at home with his mother, a senior government human resources officer, was then thought to be the best solution. Within a few days and despite a 24-hour security guard being in place, he again escaped and was reported being seen in the community. His 10-year-old sister, who had also just returned from the USA and was isolating at home, had used TikTok to alert Cayman residents that he had escaped through a bedroom window by tying bedsheets together. He was returned to isolation.

Covid-19 Timeline – Highlights

Table 1, below, summarises what was happening in Cayman through 2020, in terms of the impact it had on Cayman's residents and the steps taken to keep everyone safe. The column on the right indicates the deadliness of the first onslaught of Covid, when there was no vaccination to protect against it and it was in its most virulent form.

Table 1

2020		Worldwide deaths
Feb 25	Travel from some countries is restricted	2,766
Feb 26	One cruise ship with a person with flu symptoms is turned away	
March 13	Ban on public gatherings	5,494
March 15	Dedicated flu clinic opens	
March 16	Arrivals must isolate for 14 days	
	Schools closed Distance learning begins	
March 19	First Covid fatality (cruise ship passenger)	11,741
	Inbound flights for returning residents only (+ UK connection plane)	
March 20	Most public places and businesses closed	

2020		Worldwide deaths
March 24	Lockdown for 58 hours	19,969
March 28	Curfews – from 7 pm to 5 am Essential tasks only during the day	
March 28	Masks required for supermarkets and essential workers	
March 28	Travel to supermarkets and essential places restricted by days allocated by surname (A-K, L-Z)	
March 31	Community transfer of 1 case of Coronavirus reported (14 cases total, but 13 from isolated travellers)	
April 5	Full lockdown on Sunday	82,808
April 6	Curfew now 7pm-7am	
April 6	First repatriation flight arrives carrying Caymanian students, PPE, test kits, pharmaceuticals	
April 13	Beaches closed	131,730
April 16	Exercise allowed between 5:15 am and 6:45 pm (travelling to exercise is prohibited)	
May 16	Wearing masks becomes a legal requirement	
May 16	Beaches open for exercise	343,332

2020		Worldwide deaths
May 18	24-hour Sunday hard curfew lifted	
May 19	Construction sector reopens (milestone in terms of people getting back to paid work and as a source of government revenue)	
	No community spread cases for over one month. Covid now only in isolated travellers.	
June 7	Bars and restaurants reopen Public transport resumes Beaches open, boating allowed Gatherings up to 10 people allowed	452,801
Jun 19	Antibody testing (LFTs) begins	
Jun 20	National Emergency Operations Committee (NEOC) deactivated	524,048
Jun 21	Curfew lifted Beauty salons and childcare services reopen 'Stay home Cayman' becomes 'Stay safe Cayman'	
July 4	Gyms and schools allowed to open (many schools stay closed)	597,347
July 19	Nightclubs reopen	
July 24, 2020	No active Covid-19 cases - not even in isolation	716,204

Finally - The End of the Year 2020

At the start of 2020 it would have been virtually impossible to predict the havoc on the world that was about to be wreaked by a microscopic virus. As most of the world was gripped in fear and spent most of their year moving from one level of lockdown to another, the residents of Cayman enjoyed, save for a few weeks of 'sheltering in place', almost complete freedom to live their usual day-to-day lives. Many of us routinely checked statistics sites such as Worldometers.com to see how badly other countries were being affected. Here are some statistics taken from that website on the last day of the year, 2020. It makes for grim reading, but the main reason it is included here is for the reader to appreciate how Cayman fits into the global pandemic. A few other countries have been chosen for comparison.

Table 2

	Number of Cases	Number of Deaths	Deaths per Million Pop.	Tests per Million Pop.
World	83,422,810	1,818,857	-	-
USA	20,217,241	350,780	1,057	758,401
UK	2,432,888	72,548	1,066	800,233
Iran	1,218,752	55,095	652	89,522
Jamaica	12,793	302	102	46,438
Cayman Islands	330	2*	30*	907,496

* One death (out of two) was the cruise ship passenger - not a Cayman resident

The year ended with many countries having record numbers of COVID-19 cases, record increases in daily cases and record numbers of deaths. In December, a new variant of COVID-19 emerged in the UK and overnight Europe closed its doors to travellers. Most countries had put systems in place that restricted people's ability to mix with others, even if they were family members. In the UK, the levels of alert were tiered. On December 31st, 17 counties were on Tier 3 lockdown (Very High Alert) and 30 counties, plus all the boroughs of London, were in Tier 4 (Stay at Home). In Cayman, we gathered without fear and enjoyed the firework displays around the islands as we welcomed in the New Year.

The good news in December 2020 was that scientists around the world, who had been working around the clock since the pandemic began, had formulated vaccines capable of protecting everyone from the disease. Various versions of vaccines emerged at once, with slightly different attributes and efficacies but it seemed like, as long as we could all survive long enough to be vaccinated, we would all be safe. Plans, typically, were to administer vaccines firstly to health professionals, the old and vulnerable, and then to other front-line workers. Eventually, and we did not know how long that might be, the world would turn back to normal.

There were some fears too, and some uncertainties. Usually, vaccines take a decade to develop and test. This one took about 9 months. Some saw this as a marvel of the scientific community, while others saw it as a 'rush job', with potentially devastating consequences. Cayman's plan was to get a high proportion of the islands vaccinated, and eventually reopen the borders to tourism.

New Year's Eve Quiz

1. There were 45 countries that had 10 or fewer COVID-19 related deaths at the end of 2020.

How many of these were *not* islands? _____

2. Which venue had the larger attendance for New Year's Eve celebrations, 2020?

a) Times Square, New York City   b) Camana Bay, Grand Cayman

3. Which venue had the better fireworks display on New Year's Eve, 2020?

a) Central Park, New York City   b) 7-Mile Beach, Grand Cayman

answers on page 252

2021 The Pandemic Continues

As most of the world moved from one type of lockdown to another, life in Cayman could easily have been mistaken for normal. Behind the scenes, though, businesses were suffering, and local people dependent on cruise ship passengers and stayover tourism were feeling the impact of living in a country with closed borders. Staycations became a trend and residents of Grand Cayman became used to booking a few nights in discounted hotel rooms, or perhaps taking an opportunity to get off Grand Cayman by visiting one of the sister islands. Forward-thinking bars and restaurants tempted people out with theme nights, so that locals could have the illusion of having travelled to Morocco, Hawaii or somewhere else that was now inaccessible.

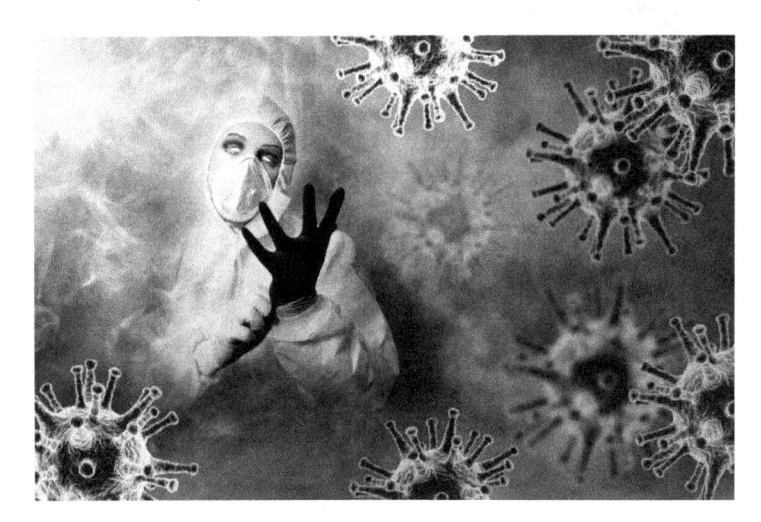

Vaccinations

Cayman did an excellent job of acquiring Pfizer vaccines and quickly set up a way of distributing them to the population. Owen Roberts Airport was an ideal site to be repurposed as a vaccination centre and by the time some countries had received their first vaccine, many of the over 50s in Cayman had received their second dose.

The initial take-up by residents seemed to indicate that everyone realised the importance of having the whole country (or at least 70%) vaccinated – it was a prerequisite for reopening the borders and restarting the local economy. However, there was an unexpected twist in the plot – with people refusing, or being so reluctant to go to be vaccinated, that there was a possibility that Cayman would squander some of its vaccines by not using them by the expiry date in June.

Various reasons were being put forward for this reluctance. One idea that was mentioned on the marl road (local vernacular for 'word on the street') was that there was a conspiracy theory involving Bill Gates and Microsoft, purporting that the vaccines placed a tracking device in people's arms. Most people considered this unlikely, as Big Tech already tracks our every thought and movement, but this was seemingly overlooked. Other people reported that some religious leaders had told their congregations not to have the vaccine, quoting religious grounds. Whatever the reason, the take-up of the vaccine had stalled. Some Members of Parliament were relatively slow to be vaccinated, with the Minister for Tourism only receiving his first dose on May 8th, 2021, according to a notice shared by Gov.ky on May 10th.

There was an epiphany of sorts when incentives were offered to those who went for their rather late, first vaccination. As the Pfizer expiry date loomed nearer, the local brewery offered a free beer, and a fast-food restaurant chain rewarded vaccine recipients with a burger. Maybe some were holding out for a bigger incentive. What could be better than a free beer and a burger? This is Cayman, remember, and to increase the uptake in vaccinations the reward was increased substantially.

In November 2021, a local woman was presented with a cheque for winning the vaccination raffle. How much did she receive?

a) CI$10,000   b) US$10,000

c) US$50,000   d) CI$100,000

answer on page 252

Testing, Testing, Testing

The Health Services Authority (HSA) of the Cayman Islands deserve massive thanks and commendation for their relentless, behind the scenes, testing programme. They became busy from the very first day that tests became available. Over a year later, when most people had stopped paying attention to daily briefings and announcements, they were still going strong. The sample of dates in the table below serves as an indication of the number of tests they were doing in July and August 2021. The table also shows how, despite travellers having to have had negative tests before departing for Cayman, a small number had tested positive every couple of days – which would have been sufficient to infect the country if the quarantine and testing regime had not been in place. A handful were even caught in the exit screening, when being tested before leaving quarantine. Bravo Doctor John Lee and his team!

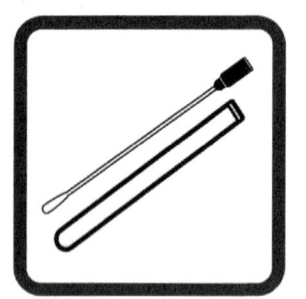

Table 3

Date	Number of Tests	Number of Positive Cases	Average Tests Per day	Arriving Traveller (T) or Community Spread (C)
May 2021	8142	41	263	41 (T)
June	8799	29	293	29 (T)
First 9 days of September (up to Phase 3)	3227	41	323	39 (T), 2 (C)

Phased Reopening Plan

In the summer of 2021, the Cayman Islands Government released a reopening plan that was intended to introduce limited tourism in September, pending the achievement of an 80% vaccination rate of the local population.

Phase 1 begun in June, and allowed entry for returning Caymanians, residents, work permit holders and others with close ties such as property owners. All travellers had to apply through the Travel Cayman portal for permission and GPS monitoring of individuals would be necessary for some. Pre-arrival PCR tests were required, as well as one before exiting quarantine. The quarantine period was 5 days for verified vaccinated people, 10 days for unverified and 14 days for unvaccinated travellers. This meant that anyone returning with small children, who would be unvaccinated, would need to stay with them for 14 days.

Phase 2 went into action as planned on the 9th of August. The main difference was that there was no requirement for GPS monitoring except for travellers ineligible for the 5-day quarantine. In a statement made on September 8th, it was made known that there had been 52 breaches of quarantine recorded in August, and that additional protocols had been introduced to reduce such events.

Phase 3 began, on schedule, on September 9th with the borders now being open for vaccinated travellers, adults, and over 12s visiting purely for leisure reasons. Quarantine periods remained the same as before, with the same exit PCR test. The main loosening of restrictions at this phase was related to the reasons for travel.

Phase 4 was the 'Reduced Quarantine Restrictions' phase. This was the major, and quite scary, reopening step, with a target date of October 14th, 2021. This phase removed quarantine restrictions for fully vaccinated travellers. This would be a large leap forward, but would increase the risk of infection transmission, as tourists would now be mingling with residents without the safety net of a quarantine period. Unvaccinated travellers would need to apply for entry through Travel Cayman and then quarantine for 14 days but verified vaccinated travellers would be free to enjoy full freedom of the islands immediately upon their arrival. Also, although it was still a requirement for vaccinated travellers to have a pre-travel PCR test, there would be no requirement for a test once they landed.

In Phase 5, scheduled for November 18th, the main change was that unvaccinated children could arrive with their verified vaccinated parents and enter the community without quarantining. Unvaccinated children over 12 would be required to quarantine for 14 days.

Finally, to be assessed on January 27th, 2022, if all had gone well the government would celebrate the Grand Re-Opening of the islands. All travellers would be welcome without quarantine or travel restrictions, including cruise ship passengers.

Phase 3 comes into Effect

Community Cases Hit the Headlines

Just two days before the scheduled reopening day, not only was there a positive case of Covid-19 in a traveller, but two community cases were picked up by the HSA. A patient with multiple medical complaints, so not presenting as a typical Covid case, was admitted to hospital, and found to be positive. Staff at the hospital, potentially exposed, were then required to isolate. A second person who tested positive and had mild symptoms was managing in isolation at home. Twenty-four close contacts of the patient were tested, including four children, two of whom had attended school for part of the day before being recalled. Thankfully all the children tested negative for the disease, but over the course of the next few days, as the schoolchildren of George Town Primary School were tested, several were found to be positive.

On the day that Cayman entered Phase 3, September 9th, 2021, a passenger who presented a positive Covid-19 test result managed to board a Cayman Airways flight from Kingston to Grand Cayman. This was only realised as the traveller was going through the arrival protocols at Owen Roberts International Airport by Customs and Border Controls (CBC) officers. The passenger and their companion were detained, and all the other passengers went into quarantine as normally required under Phase 3 but had that been Phase 4 the passenger would have gone straight from the airport into the community. There were concerns that flight attendants may have been in contact with the passenger and therefore able to spread the disease, but decisions were made that allowed the airline staff to stay out of quarantine.

Border Reopening is Paused

Reopening the borders was put on hold, before it had even begun, with Premier Panton announcing that there would be an indefinite pause in the reopening plan, and continued closure of the borders. It had only taken a couple of schoolchildren to test positive in September and the hopes of a half-decent tourist season were smashed to smithereens, and so, potentially, were livelihoods.

The Cayman Islands Tourism Association was quick to make its feelings heard, and understandably so. Many hotel and tourism operations had invested in staffing, work permits and infrastructure for reopening, and had had the rug pulled from beneath them – at great cost.   On top of that was all the lost revenue – the income that would have come from a few good months of tourism, that many needed simply to survive. Carriers, such as American Airlines, had to revise their plans too. Perhaps committing planes to a route to a country that could change its mind so readily seemed like a bad idea. Not only did they have to stop planes, due to the CI government's ban, but their confidence in the country seemed to have been diminished. They announced in October that they were not going to be resuming flights to Cayman until February 2022.

Which of these figures most closely represents the number of people who arrived by air in 2019?

A. 350, 000

B. 450,000

C. 500,000

D. 600,000

answers on page 252

Masks Back On

After over a year of freely moving around the islands without a care in the world, events in late-September and October of 2021 soon meant that residents had to start taking protection seriously and soon, seeing people wearing masks became commonplace. It did not take long before mask-wearing became mandatory in many public spaces, including schools and most workplaces.

Early incidents of note included the announcement that an unvaccinated health worker working in the screening service at Doctors Hospital had tested positive on Sept 21st.

The following week, as announced on September 28th, Public Health had found eight positive results. Four of these were in travellers and two were in households of returning travellers – which was all very ordinary. However, the bulletin also mentioned that there were two community cases including a child in Year 6 at Prospect primary school – and nobody knew the source of the infection for either of those two community cases.

Schools in Cayman had been scheduled to break up at the end of the school day on Friday 15th October and return on Monday 25th, after one week of well-earned rest. However, the outbreak of cases in schools prompted the government to close government schools early. It was not merely the presence of the disease in the schools that was responsible, but the resultant number of teachers who had to stay at home in isolation that made teaching untenable.

Many schools soon had cases, and a protocol was established of sending home the students from the affected classes and requiring their parents, and anyone else with whom they would have been in close contact, to stay home in isolation. On 14th October there were 1,247 individuals in isolation involving hundreds of households.

Vaccine Mandates become a Hot Topic

On October 5th, 2021, Members of Parliament passed two bills mandating Covid-19 vaccinations for non-Caymanians in the Cayman Islands. Anyone requiring a work permit to live in Cayman would need to show evidence of being vaccinated. It was a controversial move as it impinged on the personal rights and freedoms of individuals. There were some exceptions, and a grace period built in, but some people took to the streets to protest.

Indeed, in many countries around the world there were demonstrations and riots in the streets over mandatory 'vaccine passports' being required for workers, or for civilians to be able to use public transport or enter buildings. In Italy, demonstrations against strict vaccination rules brought together disparate groups. Anarchists, trade unionists, neo-fascists and ultra-conservative Catholics presented a united front against the government in a way that had not been seen since the 1970s.

In Cayman, the relatively small group of protesters made references to the Cayman Constitution and the United Nations Declaration of Human Rights that stipulate, among other things, that "no one shall be subjected without his free consent to medical or scientific experimentation."

Lateral Flow Testing

As schools returned after the October mid-term break there was a need for testing that could be done by individuals rather than by Public Health, which was by then under immense strain - conducting around 1000 PCR tests per day. Through good forward planning, Cayman was prepared for this, through the importation and introduction of lateral flow testing which was made widely available.

Before LFTs, if, say a schoolchild or a family member of a school child had tested positive, perhaps through community transmission, the child, his teacher, and classmates would all be sent home. However, due to the simplicity of LFTs, all these individuals could now take a test at home and return to school or work the next day if their result tested negative. Positive results would be reported to Public Health and only those individuals would need to stay home. Contact tracing would follow for them, and further tests would be forthcoming, but normal daily life could at least continue for everyone else at the child's school.

Eventually, people were administering their own LFTs once or twice per week and before going to gatherings. Children arriving at school who heard that a classmate had reported a positive result now could sit in their parents' car, do a test, and continue into school a few minutes later if their test came out negative.

1. What do the letters mean on the LFT?

S stands for _____

C stands for _____

T stands for _____

2. Explain what should be concluded if:

a) A red line appeared only against the C

b) A red line appeared next to both the C and the T.

c) No red lines appeared.

answers on page 252

238

Variants

The table (below) highlights the important dates and statistics relating to daily Covid-19 cases for 2020 and 2021. It is interesting to match the evolution of the coronavirus with statistics of its effects in Cayman.

Table 4

Date	Daily Cases in Cayman	Total Deaths
Dec 23, 2021	141	11
Dec 15th, 2021. First **Omicron variant** detected in Cayman		
Dec 8, 2021	70	9
Dec 4, 2021	85	7
Dec 1, 2021	250	6
Nov 30, 2021	336	5
Nov 17, 2021	714	4
Oct 4, 2021	52	
Sep 7, 2021	25	
Aug 1, 2021	0	
July 21st, 2021. First **Delta variant** detected in 2 vaccinated (and isolated) travellers from Miami.		
Cayman was operating covid-free but with no tourism		
Nov 17, 2020		2
July 24, 2020. Cayman curfews have stopped, and restaurants, bars, clubs, and beaches all reopen.		
Mid-March: Cayman's school closures, lockdown, and travel restrictions begin		
Mar 16, 2020		1

Reopening – Phase 4   November 2021

From 29th October 2021, Lateral Flow Tests (rapid antigen tests) were happening daily across the islands. The Phase 4 reopening of the borders, which had been planned for October, was now going forward for real in November. It meant that from November 20th, vaccinated travellers would be able to enter the country without needing to quarantine. Not only would this allow tourists in, but it would mean that residents would be able to leave the island, perhaps over the Christmas period, to go see loved ones or do some shopping, and return to their own homes. Flights, and spaces on them, were limited, but people began making travel plans. After all, in most cases, they had been marooned since March 2020.

Up to this point there had only been two deaths from Covid in over 18 months, but the week before the reopening there was a third. Everyone checked to find more details – in this case it was a 73-year-old male who was unvaccinated. It was reassuring to discover that anyone who died, or was hospitalised, was either aged or had pre-existing health problems – and preferably, not vaccinated.

Table 4 on the previous page shows the spike in cases in mid-November. This coincided with residents returning after a half-term school break. The number of cases per day then went down quite dramatically until mid-December, despite the new Phase 4 rules. The reason for this decrease was that residents who had booked to go away over the Christmas holiday period were being extra cautious. They did not dare risk catching Covid before they were due to fly. Among other things, they would have missed their vacation and probably lost money from cancelled flights and accommodations.

By this time, many countries had reduced their safety restrictions. The USA still required proof of a negative test result for inbound passengers., but those travelling to America at Christmas, say, would have been aware that many people in stores there were not wearing masks. Cayman still was playing very safe. Indeed, there was a requirement for people returning after their Christmas break to test negative for Covid within 24 hours of flying. Everyone also needed their proof of vaccination and a certificate, obtained through the Travel Cayman Portal, that showed they had permission to enter Cayman. Despite all this, there was a massive spike in Covid cases in January.

A British Airways plane arriving

Travel questions

1. Which were the only destinations available as a direct flight from Cayman in December 2021?

New York, Miami, Toronto, Dallas, Tampa, Nassau, Kingston, Chicago, Orlando, Charlotte, Fort Lauderdale, London

2. What is the name of the dive resort and bar underneath the flightpath in the photo above?

answers on page 252

Omicron

The spike in cases after the Christmas break was not simply because Cayman residents had mingled with infected people in the countries they visited, it was also because of the way Covid had evolved. When infectious diseases are so deadly that the world goes into hiding it causes a problem for the virus – it runs out of hosts. It seems that the Covid-19 virus decided on a new approach - to infect people without making the symptoms so brutal or obvious, then let them circulate amongst others for a little longer than before, and then kill fewer of them so they did not become unavailable through isolation. It worked – the new variant was more transmissible and less lethal.

The number of Omicron cases in the USA surpassed Delta cases in late December 2021, and in the UK by early January. People infected by Omicron were 50% more likely to pass it on to family members than those infected with the Delta variant, and Omicron was better at getting past the protection provided by being vaccinated. Even family members who had been triple-vaccinated had twice the risk of being infected by Omicron. These would have been alarming statistics if this variant had kept its virility, but after a while we learned that, although the number of cases was rapidly increasing, fatalities were not.

Table 5 Comparisons at notable dates during 2022

2022	Worldwide daily new cases (x million)	Cayman daily new cases*	Daily deaths worldwide*
Jun 12th	0.41	1,007	786
May 30th	0.45	841	1,662
May 10th	0.67	750	2,063
Apr 30th	0.51	478	1,788
Apr 15th	0.78	285	2,732
Apr 8th	1.1	515	4,000
Mar 31st	1.5	587 **	4,419
Mar 17th	**2.1**	96	5,650
Mar 1st	1.5	60	7,743
Feb 24th	1.8	1041	10,596
Feb 12th	2.4	1753	11,955
Feb 2nd	3.2	2146	**12,474**
Jan 20th	**3.8**	**2122**	10,996
Jan 14th	3.4	608	8,284
Jan 7th	2.8	466	6,133
Jan 1st	1.86	125	5,019

*(closest to the date for 'worldwide daily cases' column)

**(the average of 2 days' data that week)

The First Few Weeks of 2022

Table 5 on the previous page highlights the impact of travel over the holiday period, combined with the transmissibility of the new variant. Numbers of cases rose dramatically through January into February. On Monday 10th January, Cayman's Chief Medical Officer (interim), reported that there were 3,430 active cases in Cayman. Two deaths were registered that week, both were unvaccinated.

People standing in line on South Church Street, queueing for a PCR test at the South Sound Community Centre after testing positive at home on a rapid antigen test – January 2022.

Returning travellers, who had been negative on the day before travelling, were testing positive on antigen tests within a week or so of their arrival. The protocol was that they then had to go to a local clinic for a swab that would be sent to a lab for a PCR test. Clinics that had seen only a handful of positive cases coming in for PCR tests prior to the holidays, and were staffed to cope with this level, were soon overrun with the multitude of people who were testing positive at home and required by law to attend.

Table 6   Cayman Covid Cases

Date 2022	Daily new cases Cayman	Air arrivals (month)	Cruise arrivals (month)	Total Deaths
July 1	423			29
June 14	1,007	26,191	89,868	28
May 30	841		60,769	28
May 11	750			28
Apr 27	468	25,114	45,481	27
Apr 15	285			26
Apr 7	515			24
Mar 25 *	587**	22,774	**16,879**	24
Mar 11	60			24
Feb 24	645	12,271	0	24
Feb 17	**1041**			**22**
Feb 13	-			17
Feb 9	**1753**			**16**
Feb 6	**2176**			**15**
Jan 13	440	5,962	0	14
Jan 2	125			12

*average of 2 days' data

**cruise ships returned this week

By the last week of January there were over 6,000 active cases of Covid-19 across Cayman – all isolating at home. That was roughly 10% of the population. This continued through February, impacting workers in all fields. It seemed like everyone was either infected or knew several people who had Covid. Fortunately, in most cases the symptoms were like having a bad, lingering cold. Other people had no symptoms at all. The new variant was thriving. The Omicron variant's relative lack of severity lulled people into a mindset that all was well, – that we could now move around as we pleased with no consequences. Around the islands, there was still an expectation that masks should be worn in shops, supermarkets, and banks, and perhaps when in close contact with others at work, but these same people would be far more relaxed in social situations, and community spread was rife. From March to June, children and staff were getting sent home from pre-schools and schools, and most of Cayman's population suffered periods of sickness between Christmas until summer. Perhaps those who had already had Omicron may have thought that they were immune, and therefore took fewer precautions, but it turns out that those antibodies offered little protection against reinfection. One UK study reported that reinfection with an Omicron variant was eight times more likely than the same risk when Delta had been the main variant.

Another reason for community transmissions of Covid in the first few weeks of 2022 may have been that people needed to be at work. Some had used their allotted sick days, and even if they tested positive on a LFT test, they might be tempted to go to work if they were showing no symptoms. We might never know the exact number of people who were roaming the community when they should have been self-isolating.

It can be seen from Table 6 how successful the Omicron variant became in 2022. With eased restrictions and milder symptoms, the virus ran riot across Cayman for months. There were more Covid-related deaths in 2022 than in the previous 2 years combined, even though the variant was milder. By October 2022, the number of deaths attributed to Covid in the Cayman Islands was 32.

Cruise Ships

The next step and a very visual milestone in Cayman's tourism recovery, was the return of the cruise liners. From March 21st, 2022, cruise ships began to arrive in George Town. There was no government requirement for disembarking passengers to test for Covid. There were some fears that infected passengers may transmit the virus to hospitality workers, particularly taxi drivers, which would then spread through the community. Long stay tourists arriving by air and staying in hotels still needed to show evidence of a negative test before boarding for Cayman.

Disney Magic March 21st, 2022

The data in Table 6 shows that numbers of new daily cases dipped in early March then rose again and stayed that way after that. There were several factors that may have caused the number of cases. The table indicates the increases in tourist arrivals, but they do not necessarily account for higher numbers of Covid cases.

Spikes in daily cases emerged, as would have been expected, by events where people gathered in large numbers and by sudden influxes of travellers. Batabano, a huge street carnival on Grand Cayman, took place on May 7th, for instance – after which there was a jump in the figures for a few weeks. However, the residents of Cayman were willing to accept these extra cases as they were not life-threatening, and it meant that islanders could enjoy their lives again.

The June figures showed that daily cases passed the 1,000 mark again – with no mass influx of residents or annual street party to explain it. It was more likely attributable to the gradual rise in the number of tourists entering the islands.

The End is in Sight!

On June 24th, 2022, it was announced that from June 30th it would no longer be a requirement for visitors to test negative for Covid before arriving by air, and that the indoor mask mandate was to be lifted. This was only in place until the end of August, but it meant that residents would now have a much easier time coming and going over the school holiday summer period. A huge wave of relief was felt all over the islands.

A Travel Certificate issued by the Cayman Government

One remaining feature of the restrictions was that there was still a requirement to use the Travel Cayman portal – basically to seek permission to enter Cayman. Although many islanders complained that this should have also been lifted, it made sense that there should still be a tracking system - especially in the light of, potentially, a huge spike in mid-August when everyone would be returning or back from the multitude of places they would have been over the summer.

The easing of restrictions did not mean that Covid had finished, or that we humans had won the war against the virus. Indeed, within a week of the government's announcement we heard of our 29th Covid-related death.

The End

During the 2022 school summer vacation period, with thousands of Cayman residents off island, the CI Government met to consider easing restrictions down to the barest of bones. On the 19th August it was announced that people planning to return or come to Cayman no longer needed to be tested prior to travel if arriving on or after August 24th. This was a great relief to all those people, especially families, who would have had to spend valuable time and money taking rapid antigen tests in the run-up to their trip home. Other travel restrictions were also dropped. There was no longer a requirement to obtain a certificate to travel via Travel Cayman. There was no need to isolate or quarantine upon arrival and the vaccination status of travellers was no longer an issue of concern to the government.

The government had not thrown all caution to the wind, though. There was still an expectation that people would use LFT tests as and when needed to check if they had Covid. If they tested positive, they should self-isolate for seven days but there was no requirement for a person to test once isolation had been completed. Family members of those isolating could attend work or school if they, themselves, took LFTs and tested negative each day. It was still a public health requirement to report a positive lateral flow test - but it is possible that many positive results were unreported. There were now no restrictions on the number of people who could attend public gatherings.

Masks were finally off! Almost. Health centres, residential care homes, prisons and a couple of other establishments might still require a mask on entry, but everywhere else was mask-free. For instance, you would need to wear one in a doctor's clinic waiting room, or at the pharmacy, but not at the supermarket. Some banks maintained their mask-wearing entry requirements for a few weeks but soon stopped. When the 'Masks Required' signs came off the entry doors to buildings it symbolised that we had made it through the pandemic - and come out alive at the other side.

Answers for Chapter 13

Page 226   1. 37 of the 45 were islands. 8 were not: Burundi, Eritrea, Western Sahara, Monaco, Vatican City, Mongolia, Cambodia, and Bhutan

2. Camana Bay, with an estimated crowd of a few hundred, safely unmasked adults and children. There was no need for masks, as Cayman was Covid-free at the time. Although there was a 'ball drop' in NYC at midnight, only the police were present, turning would-be revellers away to the safety of their homes.

3. 7-Mile Beach. Cayman's hotels put on a good show of fireworks. Central Park's traditional firework display was cancelled because of COVID.

Page 229 $100,000

Page 234   C. 500,000 (Actually 502,739 - a record at the time)

Page 238   1. Sample, Control, Test

2. A. Negative, no Covid   B. Positive   C. Something went wrong. Try another one.

Page 241   New York, Miami, Toronto, Nassau, London (Heathrow)

Acknowledgements

Hundreds of reference sources were used in putting together this book. In most cases, several websites were cross-checked for consistency and accuracy. For instance, the National Hurricane Center might have been the first port of call for information on a tropical storm, then if the hurricane affected a specific country, the next place checked would have been that country's official website, followed by other regional sites that have a special interest in that region's weather or in tropical storm history. Having said that, it should be understood that I am not an immunologist, seismologist, pirate or entomologist, so none of what I have written in this book should be taken as expert advice.

Extreme caution was used to only include images and photographs that were in the public domain or were otherwise unrestricted for public and commercial use. I provided some of the photographs and illustrations myself.

Below is a list of some of the main resources that I would like to acknowledge and thank. There were many others and I apologise if I have missed any here.

The National Hurricane Center, Miami.

Worldometers.info

ExploreGov.ky

The Cayman Islands Government ebook: A Brief History of the Cayman Islands by David Wells of the West India Committee for the Government of the Cayman Islands

Montgomery, Marc. *A Portrait of Success: The Rise of the Cayman Island as an Offshore Financial Center*

Hannerz, Ulf 1974 *Caymanian Politics: Structure and style in a Changing Island Society*, Stockholm, Stockholm Studies in Social Anthropology

Centers for Disease Control and Prevention cdc.gov

Wikipedia.com

History.com

Nasa.com

Smithsonian Magazine

Forbes.com

nhm.ac.uk Natural History museum

livescience.com

USGS.gov United States Geological Survey

Nationalgeographic.com

Founded upon the Seas: A History of the Cayman Islands and Their Peoples - Book by Michael Craton

Caymannewsservice.com

Caymancompass.com

pexels.com

Sciencedirect.com

Coastalcare.org

The World Health Organization who.int

The Pan-American Health Organization paho.org

Other books on the Cayman Islands by John Clark:

Tales of the Cayman Islands - In Verse

The Cayman Islands - An Artist's Perspective

The Cayman Islands Colouring Book - Book One and Book Two

Book One

Book Two

About the Author

 John Clark first arrived in Grand Cayman in 1987, in the days when access to parts of 7-Mile Beach was by driving over and around sand dunes. He has been an educator in the high school sector for almost forty years, teaching: psychology, geography, history, RE, mathematics, English, and specialist programmes for children with learning difficulties. Most of his career has been spent in Cayman's schools.

John is well known in Cayman for his colourful paintings of Cayman scenes, featuring traditional Cayman houses, poincianas, bougainvillea and beach scenes. His full collection of artwork depicting Caribbean, Hawaiian and European beauty spots can be found on the Fine Art America website.

Printed in the USA
CPSIA information can be obtained
at www.ICGtesting.com
LVHW011626080924
790491LV00030B/414